HOME AND GARDEN STYLE

HOME
— AND —
GARDEN
STYLE

CREATING A UNIFIED LOOK
INSIDE AND OUT

John Brookes and
Eluned Price

WARD LOCK

First published in the UK 1996
by Ward Lock
Wellington House
125 Strand
London
WC2R 0BB

A Cassell Imprint

Distributed in the United States
by Sterling Publishing Co., Inc.
387 Park Avenue South, New York, NY 10016–8810

Distributed in Canada
by Cavendish Books Inc.
Unit 5, 801 West 1st Street
North Vancouver, B.C., Canada V7P 1PH

A British Library Cataloguing in Publication Data block for
this book may be obtained from the British Library

ISBN 0 7063 7454 1

Designed by Bernard Higton
Picture researcher: Julia Pashley
Printed in Great Britain by Bath Press Colourbooks, Glasgow

CONTENTS

Above: John Brookes' terrace in West Sussex.
Opposite: Eluned Price's conservatory in Oxford.

PREFACE

This book discusses the relationship between house and garden; it considers the ways in which the two have developed, both separately and together; and it explores our perception of that relationship today.

It has been our intention to set out the principles of such developments, relating them as far as possible to the fashions and priorities that govern design today. Rather than bowing to the accepted notion that a house is one thing and the garden a separate venture, you are invited to consider the site, the land and the building as an integrated whole.

Now that we have smaller properties and limited sites it has become even more important to use what little space we do have as well as we can – both inside and out. The concept is certainly not novel, but only recently has it become affordable for most people. We have considered the evolution of garden design from the ancient world, especially the period of the Roman Empire, because these early eras, which revealed great sophistication in both design and construction, have influenced garden layout as well as architecture in the following centuries.

The components of garden design – natural resources, construction skills, paving and plantings – have barely changed since they were first used, and the architecture of Roman villas are as sophisticated as any today. The technology may alter, but the basic intelligence and aesthetic principles remain the same.

THE ORIGINS OF INTEGRATED STYLE

The building and decorating of houses and gardens are not new. Their origins lie not only in necessity – to provide a roof over one's head and fruit and vegetables to eat – but also in the capacity for, and tendency towards, the production of art in its most general sense. It took man a good two and a half million years to progress from stone tool-making to the production of art, but for the last 35,000 or 40,000 years we have been painting and decorating ever since.

The 24,000-year-old 'finger macaroni' decorations in the Koonalda Cave, made by dragging the fingers through soft clay applied to the walls, would appear to have been made by Australia's earliest plasterers. In the northern hemisphere in the same period a more pastoral approach to wall decoration was favoured by the frescoists of the caves at Gargas and La Grèze in their representatons of deer, horses, mammoths and bison. The paintings of the Lascaux Caves are later – a mere 15,000 years old. Here a sophisticated Palaeolithic artist enhanced the images of animals and men with different shades of ochre and manganese pigments, and used the humps and hollows of the cave wall to create a three-dimensional effect. Whether these paintings have some religious import or whether they are the records of hunting triumphs or illustrations for the tuition of young braves scarcely matters from the point of view of the human capacity or urge to execute them. As Dr Schuyler Jones, Director of the Pitt-Rivers Museum, Oxford, says: 'It appears to be a universal characteristic of modern man to decorate either themselves or their belongings.'

The most fundamental change to have occurred within the last 40,000 years was the domestication of plants and animals during the Holocene era, which began some 10,000 years ago, after the

Above: Many a Mediterranean villa is built into older farmed terraces, of vine or of olive. This Riviera example sits in just such a location.

Right: Square panes and the delicate tracery of wrought iron are the perfect frame for the curves of the formal garden at Easton Neston, Northamptonshire.

last glaciation. Until then man was a nomadic hunter-gatherer and scavenger. With the cultivation of crops, which began in the Middle East, man's problems began. For once humans began to grow food, they needed to create stable communities, which meant permanent settlements, and given man's predisposition to art and decoration, home and garden style can be said to have begun.

In this introduction we are going to look at the origins of an integrated style for a number of different reasons. First, because we intend to show that houses and gardens and their interrelationship are not just a discovery of modern times. The technology and the detail may change according to the sophistication of the society, but they cannot be said to progress in a strictly linear sense. Our cities and our public and private gardens are different from those of the Romans but they are not necessarily more beautiful or more intelligently planned. Far from it. The second reason is that an integrated style was, until recent times and for obvious reasons, a concept limited to warmer climates. The third reason is simply that this is not the place for a long and detailed history of house and garden design – apart from those earlier civilizations in more temperate climes, they proceeded separately and are not therefore the proper subject of an essay on integration.

According to the Bible, Man is primarily a gardener: 'And the Lord God took the man, and put him into the Garden of Eden to dress it and keep it.' More than 150 plants – trees, herbs and flowers – are mentioned in the Bible. There are commandments governing the preservation of trees and injunctions against cropping young fruit trees too early. St Paul talked about grafting and the right stock for fruit trees. Mary mistook the risen Christ for the gardener. Much of the imagery in the Bible is drawn from nature and husbandry, with the garden as a distinct and separate concept. Isaiah used all three as metaphors. So did Solomon, who 'made me gardens and orchards' and they were scented, his 'fountain of gardens': he called upon the north and south winds to 'blow

upon my garden, that the spices thereof may flow out'. Royalty, of course, fared better than most from the house and garden point of view. In the Book of Esther the king gave a banquet, lasting for seven days, for the people of Susa:

in the court of the garden of the king's palace. There were white, green and blue hangings, fastened with cords of fine linen and purple to silver rings and pillars of marble ... upon a pavement of red and blue and white and black marble.

What is interesting about this, and we shall see it again and again, is that the civilizations of more temperate climates developed concepts of inside–outside living quite naturally. Their gardens, or at least those areas nearest the house, were taken as extensions of indoor living. In hot climates this is entirely logical. To escape from the suffocating heat of an interior without the benefit of air-conditioning, built albeit with thick walls to deflect the heat of the sun, the move to verandas and to courtyards shaded by vines and figs and cooled by the play of water is both necessary and natural.

In less temperate areas the need for the creation of outdoor 'rooms' did not arise. Quite the opposite, in fact. The curious buttress-like constructions that can be seen along the length of an eighteenth- or nineteenth-century wall are chimneys for the furnaces that heated the wall on which peaches and other fruits were grown. When Palladianism took root in Britain in the eighteenth century and classical villas, similar to those designed by Palladio in the sixteenth century for northern Italy, began to be built, Lady Mary Wortley Montagu appositely remarked that they were 'perfectly contrived for the coolness agreeable in Italy but killing in the North of England'.

The Minoan and Mycenaean civilizations of the Aegean can be said to have laid the groundwork for modern architecture, despite the constant earthquakes. The Minoan palaces of Knossos and Phaistos on Crete are the earliest examples of European architecture, built to replace those lost in the earthquakes of c.1700 BC. These later palaces

Frescoes, dating from c.1500 BC, in the southwest room of Knossos Palace, Crete. The solid simplicity of the architecture is offset by the sophistication of the murals.

were carefully integrated with the landscape, with hanging gardens, colonnaded walks and courtyards. No one visiting Knossos can fail to be moved by the familiarity of the detail: the dado and fragile decoration above it, the queen's apartments, with a fresco of dolphins frolicking in the sea spray surrounded by flying fish, a clay bathtub in a small room off, and, along the corridor, another room with the lavatory still *in situ*, but now without its wooden seat or connection to the palace's elaborate plumbing system.

After the decline of Crete from c.1400 BC the Mycenaeans' superior engineering skills, monumental planning and sophisticated taste produced the fortified acropolis as the civic and religious centre of the city, an architectural development epitomized by the citadel of Mycenae itself, with its majestic walls, its courtyards, staircases and rooms arranged on a single axis, and its stone sculptures, paintings and encrustations of alabaster. They bequeathed to Greek architecture the acropolis and the megaron – a rectangular room, usually with four columns supporting the roof and a central hearth, whose lateral walls extended to form the sides of an external colonnaded porch or portico. The megaron was possibly the forerunner of the Greek temple.

Of the buildings on the Acropolis at Athens, Plutarch wrote that 'they were created in a short time for all time'. And the Parthenon remains the most nearly perfect building ever created, a tribute to the philosophical, mathematical and aesthetic ideals of Greece and her architects. The Greek concern with proportion led them to develop a theoretical basis for their art, and in the fifth century BC the sculptor Polyclitus expounded his theory of *symmetria*, which centred on the commensurability of parts of the body. This principle governed all Greek art and architecture, from the shape of vases, the articulation of the decoration on them, the stance of a statue and its size, to the pediments of the Parthenon.

The greatness of Greek architecture was confined to their public and religious buildings. Domestic buildings, for socio-political reasons, were immeasurably simpler. The vitality of the *polis* (city-state) depended on public, or civic, life, which was conducted only by male citizens. Women were strictly segregated and rarely left the home. By contrast with the magnificent buildings intended for oratory and debate, festivals and games, the Athenian home was mean and unimpressive, nor did the citizen of the *polis* display a lifestyle that was markedly different from that of any other citizen. Only in the Hellenistic period (323–27 BC), as a wealthy middle class began to emerge, did houses begin to acquire some architectural pretensions. A typical middle-class house in Priene or Delos, for example, centred on a small court and had at least one large reception room, opening from the north side of the peristyle to catch the winter sun. There might be statues or marble furnishings set in the colonnades, and inside there would be mosaic flooring and painted stucco wall decorations.

The arts and architecture of domestic life in ancient Rome represent the apotheosis of civilization. The empire, or at least the wealthy citizens of the empire, enjoyed most of the trappings of civilized life we have today – central heating, superior internal plumbing systems and a great deal of glass. The drawbacks were much the same. A rapidly increasing population led to high-rise apartment blocks: in *De Architectura* (before AD 27) the architect Vitruvius Pollio refers to tower blocks with fine views. In the first century Juvenal wrote in despair of the crumbling tenements of the poor, and Augustus was obliged, for safety reasons, to limit their height to 21 metres (70 feet). But there were also planned shop- and apartment-blocks, as at Herculaneum, and at Ostia there were apartment-blocks of five or six rooms linked by a wide corridor. Nero's excesses included the suburbanization of 140 hectares (350 acres) at the heart of Rome for a palace complete with artificial landscape and ornamental lake. Suetonius railed: 'All Rome is transformed into a villa!' Seaside resorts for the wealthy proliferated, and in vain did Horace (65–68 BC) inveigh against the fashionable villas of Baiae, which threatened to remodel the coastline.

Pliny the Younger (AD 62–113) took a huge delight in the design of his villas and their gardens. He understood as well as we do now the importance of suiting a building to its landscape. His villa at Laurentum:

> opens into a hall, unpretentious but not without dignity, and then there are two colonnades, rounded like the letter D, which enclose a small but pleasant courtyard. This makes a splendid retreat in bad weather, being protected by windows and still more by the overhanging roof. Opposite the middle of it is a cheerful inner hall, and then a dining room which really is rather fine: it runs out towards the shore and ... has folding doors or windows as large as the doors all round, so that at the front and sides it seems to look out on to three seas. ... Round the corner is a room built round in an apse to let in the sun as it moves round and shines in each window in turn, and with one wall fitted with shelves like a library to hold the books which I read and read again.

On the second storey were two living rooms and another dining room, 'which commands the whole expanse of sea and stretch of shore with all its

lovely houses'. In addition to the bathroom, which was 'fitted with two curved baths built out of opposite walls', and two rest rooms, 'beautifully decorated in a simple style', was a heated swimming pool, 'which is much admired and from which swimmers can see the sea. Close by is the ball court which receives the full warmth of the setting sun'.

The garden was designed to take account of its coastal situation: 'All round the drive runs a hedge of box, or rosemary to fill any gaps, for box will flourish extensively where it is sheltered by the buildings, but dries up if exposed in the open to the wind and salt spray even at a distance.' Inside the inner ring of the drive was a young and shady vine pergola. In addition to a 'well-stocked kitchen garden', the main garden, 'thickly planted with mulberries and figs', was a covered arcade, with windows on both sides but more facing the sea', and in front a terrace 'scented with violets'.

The situation of his country house at Tifernum in Tuscany made a more elaborate garden possible. Enclosed by a drystone wall and hidden by a box-hedge planted in tiers, it had a terrace in front of the colonnade laid out with box hedges clipped into different shapes:

> from which a bank slopes down, also with figures of animals cut out of box facing each other on either side. On the level below there waves – or ripples – a bed of acanthus.

There was a court shaded by four plane trees, at its centre a fountain playing in a marble basin, overlooked by a room painted with a fresco 'of birds perched in the branches of trees'. The riding ground ran through a garden enclosed by plane trees supporting a screen of ivy. There were roses, box shrubs clipped to form Pliny's name and that of his gardener, box obelisks alternating with fruit trees and grass lawns. At the upper end was a 'curved dining seat of white marble shaded by a vine trained over four slender pillars of Carystian marble'. In front of the seat a polished marble basin acted as a dining table: its rim was wide enough to support the main dinner dishes while

the lighter ones floated on the water. Not only was there a large fountain opposite but 'by every chair a tiny fountain'. It was Pliny's descriptions of his gardens that inspired the box parterres and topiary of the sixteenth century.

For all its elaboration, it was probably executed with excellent taste. Pliny scorns his opponent at the Bar, the loathsome Regulus, not only for malpractice but also for his vulgar horticultural pretensions: 'In his gardens beyond the Tiber ... he has covered a vast area with immense colonnades and littered the bank with his precious statues.'

One of the most interesting features of the urban Roman villa of the rich was that its entrance hall was designed to run right through from the front to the back, so that anyone entering the house would immediately have a glimpse of the garden beyond. The Roman concept of integrating the house and garden was, in many respects, ahead of ours. Their

furnishings were, like our own, utilitarian and aesthetic but to a far higher standard. If the garden furniture was often marble or at least stone – for many dinner parties were held outside – interior furniture was yet more precious.

Tables in both bronze and marble, round or rectangular, were supported by elaborate legs of lions' paws, volutes or griffins. Couches were mainly of wood and cushioned, and these have, of course, largely perished, but their bronze fittings remain – elegant, lathe-turned legs, headboard ornaments of busts or horses' heads, and railings inlaid with silver, tortoiseshell or ivory. A wooden cupboard with panelled folding doors found at Herculaneum is touching in the familiarity of its design. Even that favourite suburban feature the standard lamp was seen in Roman houses. One from Pompeii is a square column standing on a plinth supported by claw feet. From each of its four scrolled and spiralling bronze branches hangs an oil-filled lamp.

Walls were either striped, panelled or plain or decorated with frescoes, such as the trellised garden mural of the house known as Livia's Villa at Primaporta, Rome. No self-respecting villa would be without its picture gallery – idyllic landscapes worthy of Claude Lorrain or reproductions of Greek masterpieces depicting momentous mythological events. Usually they were incorporated as painted panels, but Pliny had portraits hanging in his study. He also collected antiques and was particularly pleased with a Corinthian bronze statuette of an old man.

The decline of the Roman civilization was the beginning of the Dark Ages, and it was not until the Italian Renaissance, when the arts of the ancient world were rediscovered, that domestic architecture and garden design received a new impetus, derived from their long-forgotten past. But it is at this point, when the past was being recalled, that the picture bifurcates, for it was not all rediscovered at the same time.

The work of Andrea Palladio (1518–80) was a crystallization of the ideas of the High Renaissance, the influences of Michelangelo, Bramante, Sanmichele and the Byzantine architecture of Venice, and his own studies of *De Architectura*, Vitruvius' treatise on the architecture of ancient Rome. In Palladio's designs we see the revival of Roman symmetrical planning and the use of harmonic proportions, which the ancient Greeks and Romans believed described not only architectural perfection but also the beauty of the universe in terms of the mathematical principles underlying musical proportions. Palladio's 'trademark' – ruthlessly symmetrical planning – was incorporated in all his villas: a central block, decorated with a portico and flanked by long, horizontal or curving wings. He composed every conceivable variation on the theme – La Rotonda at Vicenza, for example, is a central block with hexastyle porticoes on all four sides. His use of two-storey colonnades, screens of arches and

temple-front porticoes for houses and the flying spiral staircase gave his Romanesque buildings an unprecedented grandeur and airy elegance. Palladio, however, makes no mention of either furnishings or garden design.

At first, Palladio's influence on architecture in England was reflected only in the work of Inigo Jones (1573–1652), whose work included the Queen's House, Greenwich, and the Banqueting Hall at Whitehall. Palladio's greatest influence on English architecture had to await the travels of Lord Burlington in the eighteenth century. In contrast, Pliny's garden descriptions found favour much earlier, as Sir Philip Sidney's *Arcadia*, published in 1590, with its passages lifted from Pliny makes clear.

While the fall of the Roman Empire marked the beginning of the Dark Ages in western Europe, in the south of Europe, especially Spain, Roman classical style had already fused with that of the Islamic world. The balance of the Roman layout became overlaid by an equally geometric garden concept, the result being that in many a formal Moorish patio, the surrounding columns are of Roman origin. The climate of those areas of southern Europe invaded by the Moors permitted the introduction of eastern design concepts, exemplified by the Alhambra in Granada, which was built between 1354 and 1391. Cool water canals run into summer pavilions, tinkling fountains cool the air, there are patterned tiles everywhere, and all is overlaid by the fragrance of citrus blossom. Is one inside or out? This is surely the ultimate in early inside–outness.

That these sensuous creations existed cannot have escaped the Christian world, but they were considered heathen, even disturbing in their voluptuousness, and therefore little credited as a factor in the emergence of an early Italian Renaissance style of garden whose influence was claimed as almost entirely Roman.

In fourteenth-century Italy gardens were small, flat and almost entirely inward looking. In country houses they functioned as a summer room outside.

Opposite: The Court of Lions in the Alhambra, begun in 1377. The movement of water in its four channels towards the centre and out again suggests the Islamic concept of expansion and contraction.

Some of the gardens of the Villa La Pietra date from the seventeenth century, although the villa is mostly the creation of Harold Acton in the twentieth century. The feeling is, however, pure Renaissance in the theatricality of its terraces, steps and landings.

City gardens, in Rome or Florence say, were little more than cloistered courtyards, letting in light throughout the building. Although they were integrated with the buildings that encompassed them, stylistically, they were merely infilling.

By the fifteenth century Italian Renaissance gardens had become more architectural and had introduced changes of level, retained by walls and balustrades, with the result that steps became a common feature. Water gushed and fell down the levels to cool the summer air. These were strongly architectural layouts, linked to the house that stood in their midst by views and axes that divided the gardens into rooms of classic symmetry. From early engravings we can see that structure dominated the layout. Only later were ilex and cypress planted to give much needed green shade and to soften what must have been extraordinarily rigid designs. The lofty roomed houses that stood

at their centre were surrounded by terraces from which the garden pattern flowed, with a transitional loggia or arcade often providing the link between inside and out.

Early French gardens were small, intimate enclosures based on Roman gardening theory, *Opus Ruralium Commodorum* having been translated in 1373. The illustrations of *Les Très Riches Heures* (1416) show walled enclosures divided into rectangular beds surrounded by trellis arbours of vine, honeysuckle, jasmine, hop and rose. The shift to an architectural emphasis came with the publication in 1485 of Leon Battista Alberti's *De Re Aedificatoria*, which revived interest in the work of Vitruvius and the concept of harmony. Alberti's work, together with later publications by Italians working in France, showed patterning for parterres and dictated the prototype of the formal enclosure on level ground and framed by trees as a foreground to the architecture of the building behind it, integration being visual rather than physical. Such is the early layout of the gardens of Fontainebleau, designed by André Le Nôtre (1613–1700) for Louis XIV before Versailles became the king's all-consuming passion. Rather than the strict geometry of the Italian clipped hedge, more flowing patterns of the parterre then emerged in the French garden, with beds of turf or box against a background of coloured earth known as *parterre de broderie*.

Slowly water became part of the topography of French gardens through Italian influences, although its usage was on a larger scale than in Italy, with flatter sheets of water in canals or lakes in response to the flatness of northern France. The French garden reached its apogee with Versailles, immaculately designed and executed by Le Nôtre for Louis XIV.

The development of the early English garden had parallels with both the French and Italian forms, but always on a much smaller scale and therefore with a far closer relationship to the house. In the early sixteenth century, for example, gardens were often enclosed by the wings of the house. Earlier

A garden outside Aix-en-Provence in the south of France, although it is in the pure style of northern France in the seventeenth century. Smaller and more human than its exemplar, it is, nevertheless, meticulous in its geometry.

recorded forms were usually in association with cloistered monasteries, which grew a wide variety of herbs and vegetables to support their communities. Flowers, too, were grown to adorn the altar, and there are also records of actual pleasure gardens.

In the early sixteenth century the English formal garden is usually presented as a square divided into quarters with a central fountain, each quarter being planted with open or closed knots – as opposed to parterres – of clipped herbs intertwined with box or of box alone. Their design was still French but the English interpretation of the pattern was more geometric, influenced perhaps by the maze pattern (which was said to confuse the Devil, who moves only in straight

lines), and had a unique English overlay of painted wood heraldic decoration. Such a garden – a reconstruction by Sylvia Landsberg – has been established behind Tudor House in the old part of Southampton. It dates from between 1520 and 1554. Formal bed are edged with low painted railings and punctuated by mounted wooden heraldic beasts.

The formal gardens of seventeenth-century England were increasingly influenced by French garden design. The French had by now modified their formal layout by extending the central axis by tree plantings to form the avenue, an axial approach strengthened by canals, which the English adopted with enthusiasm. Celia Fiennes, who made a number of journeys on horseback

between 1685 and 1712, recorded her impressions in a journal, and she disapproved of what she saw: 'Rows of trees paled in gravel walks, fine cut hedges, flower pots on walls, terraces, statues, fountains, basins, grass squares and exact uniform plots.' The formal garden scene was now set for a new, more liberal and humanist approach to the garden represented by nature, though in an equally controlled form.

The English landscape movement of the eighteenth century, fathered by William Kent (1685–1748), who was succeeded by Lancelot (Capability) Brown (1715–83) and Humphrey Repton (1752–1818), was not concerned with the integration of house with garden in the formal idiom but with vistas of idealized rolling English landscape that might be seen on a walk or a ride through grounds. Later however, Repton included elements of formality, again close to the house, re-introducing terraces with balustrades and steps or trellised enclosures for flowers, for he was leading the way for the restoration of a degree of formality within the garden – for throughout the eighteenth century there had been a school of thought that lamented the formal gardens that Capability Brown had destroyed.

This period of garden history is somewhat confused, because overlaying a divergence of style – the 'gardenesque', the rustic, the Italianate and so on (all of which were considered perfectly valid) – was an increasing and voracious appetite by horticulturists for exotic plants. Most of these divergent styles did, however, begin to include a transition between home and garden in the plan. The terrace and the loggia were fashionable, and, with the abolition of a tax on glass in 1845, the greenhouse and then, more importantly, the conservatory became an essential adjunct to every Victorian home.

With the developing interest in exotic plants, bedding out became popular. This was a method of planting up beds throughout the summer months to achieve as great a contrast in colour and foliage form as possible. Bedding systems were

Right: Often considered the culmination of Edwin Lutyens' collaboration with Gertrude Jekyll, the garden at Hestercombe, Somerset, was built between 1904 and 1909. Its architectural geometry is mellowed by perennial and shrubby planting of mainly introduced species.

Left: The English landscape movement is characterized by rolling parkland landscape that seems to run up to the walls of the Palladian house in its midst.

replaced by a new device known as carpet bedding, by which foliage plants were clipped flat into such patterns as that of a floral clock.

By the 1870s there was a growing reaction to such gross artificiality, and a new vogue began for the use of old-fashioned flowers. There was also a re-emergent interest in herbs. In 1870 William Robinson published his *Wild Garden*, which advocated the placing of exotic plants where they could thrive without further care. Robinson's theories reached a wider audience when he established a new journal called *The Garden*, which he also edited until 1899, when he was succeeded by Gertrude Jekyll. (In 1927 *The Garden* became *Homes and Gardens*.)

Only with the rise of a Victorian middle class and comparatively smaller gardens did the garden begin to work as an extension of living accommodation. Victorian painters of gardens give an insight into the development of the smaller garden, on the one hand as a structured imitation of grander examples and as a glorification of

Folly Farm near Reading, Berkshire, was designed by Edwin Lutyens in the Arts & Crafts idiom between 1906 and 1912. It is a garden of compartments, vistas, levels, steps, water, paving and exuberant planting.

cottage gardens on the other, paralleling the Arts & Crafts movement. The concept of the garden being an extension of the house was embodied in the partnership of Gertrude Jekyll and Edwin Lutyens who from the turn of the century together saw the garden as flowing from the building, providing a complementary experience to the interior of the building rather than being a different one. The transition from in to out goes through the conservatory, over the veranda and beneath the pergola, forcing the design to work on a domestic level.

In the same era, Beatrice Parsons in America showed vistas, pergolas, ruined walks and topiary but always with an abundance of annual planting and floriferous perennials, a form of gardening that requires great expertise in order to support its effect through the seasons. Jekyll's American counterpart, Beatrix Farrand, was also to bring structured design to the foreground. Both Parsons and Farrand produced work in smaller spaces and both influenced the philosophy of a garden that flowed from a building and provided a complementary experience to the interior of that building rather than being a different one.

As a reaction against the artificiality of Victorian garden layouts, their clashing colours and the high cost of the labour required to maintain them, the return to cottage gardening favoured by the Arts & Crafts movement, with softer colours and the use of perennials, was and is immensely popular. We have slithered into a retrogressive design mode, based largely on old world values, with heady overtones of a more romantic style. It is a mode that we in Britain seem to find hard to shake off.

From the beginning of the twentieth century the Modern Movement radically affected the design world. The horticulturist might think that this is irrelevant, but the flow of space from inside to out is a design concern, and the art of design must not be confused with the craft of gardening.

The school of arts and crafts that was established in Weimar in 1919, the Bauhaus, sought to solve what Walter Gropius, who was its founder, called

Above: The modular system of building the Japanese home, and its clean, simple lines influenced the architects of the new Modern Movement.

Right: An early twentieth-century English interpretation of the traditional Japanese garden at Compton Acres in Dorset.

'the ticklish problem of combining imaginative design with technical proficiency', by setting up workshops purposely to create well-designed articles of mass-production. The teaching at the Bauhaus effected a revolution in art education and perception – every student was involved in the design and then in the manufacture of artefacts under the umbrella of the development of new, 'rational' architecture.

The Modern Movement was much influenced by Japanese concepts. When Japan was finally opened up to foreigners in 1854 Japanese gardens became fashionable in the West, but often it was more the 'hardware' that was exported – red bridges, teahouses and the plants themselves – rather than the sophisticated and symbolical design concepts. Dry gravel gardens in the inner cloister, sliding

Surely the house to end all houses when it comes to integrating building with landscape – Fallingwater, 1936, by Frank Lloyd Wright. On each level, glazed rooms open to cantilevered balconies, which hang out over the crashing waters below.

paper doors on to verandas built to take advantage of a borrowed landscape (the principle of *shakkei*), the placement of rocks and pebbles and water to denote tranquillity in the garden used for the tea ceremony – all these concepts did not migrate to the West until the twentieth century. What was impressive was not only their flexibility – with screens used to open and close rooms, to bring in the garden or change a view – but the fact that the houses were based on a modular unit derived from their standard mat (or *tatami*) size. Anything modular, of course, interested the mass-producer.

Modernism was a watershed in design terms, for its message was no longer classic. We were now more aware of asymmetry, even abstraction, and for the first time the twentieth-century designer, whether inside or out, had a choice in the forms of his or her designs. It had never happened before. Add to this an increasing range of building materials and technologies for their construction, and you produce a cacophony of visual styles. With the great range and flexibility of different materials and technologies of the twentieth century, the feasibility of consciously designing the inside to take account of out, and outside to be seen as part of in, becomes possible. The most

Above: Philip Johnson's Glass House, New Canaan, Connecticut, built in 1949, achieves a virtually seamless sweep between in and out through the use of level surfaces, non-intrusive supports and minimal furnishings.

Opposite: A late twentieth-century interpretation of the integrated theme by Raymond Hudson in South Africa. Swimming pool, terrace and building are moulded together in one bold design, all coloured the same, and then overlaid by abundant planting. It's the Lutyens-Jekyll approach, but updated.

obvious expression of this conscious manipulation of potential was Philip Johnson's house at New Canaan, Connecticut, which he built for himself in 1949. The concept was wholly romantic, but the materials and construction techniques were contemporary. A cube of completely glazed walls, it sits in the centre of magnificent trees and park land, illuminated at night. Not for nothing is Johnson credited with the invention of the term 'international style'. The designs carried out in the house and outside are simultaneously visible because of the nature of the materials: the glass house is thus the ultimate example of cohesion between interior and landscape design.

International style also borrows from Moorish Spain with the patio (Spanish for courtyard) exemplified in the Patio de los Narajos in Cordoba. A cloistered building looks into a space divided into rectangles and planted with orange trees, all connected at their bases by narrow irrigation channels fed by the overflow from the fountain. You can almost hear the water, feel the turgid heat and smell the heavy fragrance of orange blossom. It is this essence of summer that the sun-starved northerner tries to recreate over and over again on

the terrace surrounding his house. Substitute the Moorish irrigation channel for a swimming pool and you have the essence of a twentieth-century garden in the hotter parts of the world.

Other horticultural influences have overlaid this concept of outdoor living, particularly in Britain, but its strengths and logic underpin all subsequent design fads. We now have another way to design and think about outside spaces. How we subsequently plant or style them is immaterial. As long as we get the lines and proportions correct, the room we have created outside will work both for the people who use it, with the house it surrounds, and in the environment in which it sits.

The Romans saw the garden as another space for living, holding their dinner parties outside on marble seats and couches under a vine-draped pergola or peristyle, lit by lamps and accompanied by the play of both fountains and music, their taste reflected outside as well as in by their choice of statuary. So do we. The technology may have altered, but the principle remains the same. We have come full circle. It just took us a long time to get there.

The room has now been placed in the garden. Paved, sunken and ceilinged over by a shady tree, it is the ultimate in outdoor rooms, although possible only in a hot climate, in this case South Africa. It was designed by Felicity Mullen.

CASE STUDIES

CLASSIC STYLE

When we talk about re-creating the classical look we are not talking about re-creating a full-scale version of a first-century AD villa, even though it would, if one had the money and time, be the greatest fun to re-create Pliny's villa, with its colonnades, terraces, arcades and gardens, heated swimming pool and suites of dining rooms and living rooms, all built to take advantage of the sun, the sea on three sides and the woods and mountains beyond.

If one were simply to re-create a Roman garden, without the backdrop of peristyle, Corinthian columns, mosaic floors and so forth, it would not, in fact, be immediately recognizable as such. Long, low hedging of box and rosemary, pergolas shaded by vines, topiary balls, pyramids and animals, trellises running with climbers, terracotta pots and swagged urns are all so familiar in our gardens today that no one on first entering this shrine to classical horticulture would exclaim: 'Oh how wonderful: a genuine Roman garden.'

The odd thing is that if you were to create the ruins of a Roman garden – in the manner of a Piranesi sketch – it would be recognized as such at once: a broken, fallen column here, fragments of tessellated floors there, the remnants of a box-edged walk, over-grown vines and figs falling into a decayed pool and at the back of the loggia, the merest hint of a crumbling fresco that suggests in once-vibrant colour the sports and sustenance of the gods. More usually, however, creating the classical look means picking up some of the themes of the neo-classical movement of the eighteenth century, themes that drew on Palladio's works for inspiration. The great exponents of the early phase of neo-classicism in Britain were Lord Burlington, Colen Campbell, James Gibbs, William Kent, John Vardy and Wood the Elder.

The Palladian movement really began with the publication of Colen Campbell's *Vitruvius Britannicus* (1712) and the building of Wanstead House (since demolished), London, which he began in the same year. He remodelled Burlington House, London, and designed Mereworth Castle, Kent, in the style of Palladio's rotunda. He is best known for Houghton Hall, Norfolk, and for Stourhead, Wiltshire (1721), which, together with the Arcadian landscape laid out by Henry Hoare II between 1741 and 1780 with its lake, temples and follies, represents one of the most perfect examples of Palladianism.

The latter half of the eighteenth century is characterized by a simplicity and elegance, a paring down of ornamentation or at least a unity of style of ornament. This period was dominated by the work of Robert Adam, Henry Holland, James Stuart and Nicholas Revett, John Wood the Younger and James Wyatt.

Neo-classicism was architecture's contribution to the Age of Reason, epitomized in philosophy, science and mathematics by the quest for the underlying laws of nature. In art and architecture it embodied, in the words of Johann Joachim Winckelmann, 'noble simplicity and calm grandeur'. Palladio's villas in the Veneto so impressed Lord Burlington that he returned to London in 1715 with a collection of Palladio's original drawings, which he copied and circulated. Thus was the neo-classical movement born, and it spread rapidly through Burlington's enthusiasm and his own work – he designed his own Villa Rotonda at Chiswick.

It was by no means a pure style. Although it was to some extent a reaction against the excesses of the baroque and rococo movements on the continent of Europe, which had had some influence in England, it

Above right: Hyde Park, the Roosevelt mansion, sits proudly above the Hudson River in New York State. Its siting and the stark junction between structure and site is pure American 'classic revival'.

Below right: Country comfort is combined with the proportions and architectural features of grander Palladian houses in this folly, built by Thomas Wright (1810–87) in the mid-eighteenth century.

contained elements of both. Rococo, characterized by a light, airy, delicate but intricate elaboration, found its way now into the gilded or painted carving and plasterwork that decorated wall panels, cornices, ceilings, mirrors, chimney pieces and door cases. The fretwork that was fashionable in the chinoiserie element of rococo style found its place in the reinventions of Chinese Chippendale. Palladio's designs had not included any designs for furniture, and it was, therefore, largely a question of making it up as they went along. The unique hybrid known as English Palladianism thus came into being.

Robert Adam's work was even more hybrid. His inspiration was Roman – he and his brothers John and James travelled extensively in Italy – but it is an amalgam of Greek, Roman, Hellenistic and Etruscan, Italian cinquecento and English Palladian. He mixed Greek anthemion friezes with pilaster capitals from Diocletian's palace at Spalato (Split) for the door cases at Saltram House, Devon, and old Lansdowne House, London; he used Le Roy's engravings of the Erechtheion, Athens, as a basis for his enriched gilded volutes of the Ionic columns and transferred their necking to the frieze of the entablature in the anteroom at Syon House, near London, and borrowed wholesale from the paintings and illustrations of Piranesi and Bartoli. By 1772 the Adam brothers vaunted the defeat of Palladianism: 'the massive entablature, the ponderous compartment ceiling, the tabernacle frame ... are now exploded.' In their place they had introduced a 'beautiful variety of light mouldings gracefully formed and delicately enriched' capturing 'the beautiful spirit of antiquity ... novelty and variety'.

Robert Adam's innovations were essentially decorative. The exterior designs remained Palladian although in their composition they embody the Adam theory of

The symmetry of a Georgian door case, outside, is echoed, inside, by the pier glass and console table.

movement, the 'rising and falling, advancing and receding [that] have the same effect in architecture [as] hill and dale, foreground and distance ... have in landscape'. Their work was a compromise between classicism and romanticism.

It was also a transition – between English Palladianism and the greater purity of the Greek Revival. In 1758, the year Robert Adam established himself as an architect in London, James 'Athenian' Stuart, who had returned from four years in Greece in 1755, designed the Temple at Hagley, the first building in Europe to imitate Doric style. This building was to set the pace for purity and severity and ultimately an architecture based on pure geometrical form – cube, pyramid, cylinder and square – demonstrated in France by the extreme and severest interpretations of neo-classicism by Claude Nicolas Ledoux in the Hôtel Thélusson and the theatre at Besançon. Those of Ledoux's works that survive, like the Paris toll house, Barrière de la Villette, are less extreme.

Palladianism travelled fast to the New World, as was remarked in 1720: 'There is no fashion in London but in three or four months is to be seen in Boston.' The best known of the American exponents of the Greek revival is Benjamin Henry Latrobe (1764–1820), with his stone-vaulted interiors for the Capitol. Baltimore Cathedral is probably the finest example of his work.

Stuart went on to publish the first accurate survey of ancient Greek architecture, the first volume of *The Antiquities of Athens* appearing in 1762, the second in 1789. Among his best works in the meanwhile were the ornamental buildings for the park at Hagley Hall, West Midlands, and Shugborough, Staffordshire, and several of the most important rooms in Spencer House, 'the finest town house in London', and the first properly neo-classic interiors in Britain. 'Bob the Roman' Adam was livid with jealousy. Spencer House, he declared was 'pityfulissimo'. The ceilings may be 'Greek to the teeth … but by God they are not handsome'. His dismissal of the man he derided as the 'Archipeligan Architect' was ill-founded, but the full flowering of the Greek Revival had to wait until the turn of the century.

Like every other historical style, one can suggest a flavour of the Palladian without recourse to devout exactitude. Inside a modern house, a series of broken pediments and rudimentary columns will evoke the style with a light and amusing touch, all infinitely more effective than panelling every wall and door, garnishing it with friezes and entablatures and stocking the room with reproduction furniture and marbling everything else in sight. Investing in one genuine mirror with its original gilding, albeit flaking, with bits broken off, and the silvering foxed, looks better and is a better investment than any reproduction, or once genuine piece that is now a victim of 'gold' spray.

When it comes to the garden, unless you have boundless acres to conjure with, you have a problem because the archetype of English Palladianism was the big house surrounded by a rolling landscape, in which, if you walked far enough, you would come across a temple overlooking a lake, an obelisk on a mound and a balustraded bridge from which you might glimpse the eye-catcher on the opposing hill. This has very little do with the real gardens of ancient Rome. Their private gardens surrounded the house, and they understood more than a little about creating an integration between the inside and the outside. All Pliny's villas were built to take account of their settings and benefit from them.

The English eighteenth-century revision produced what we call a classic eighteenth-century landscape, but was in no way classic in its own right. Ironically, the gardens of the previous century with their symmetry, their formal layouts, the geometry of their walks edged with low box, and their controlled vistas ending in a stop of statuary, hard stone bench or urn were far more authentically classic than the 'improvements' of the English landscape movement.

To understand how this happened you have to go back to the Italian Renaissance when horticultural contrivances reflected the will of wealthy princedoms, at a time when power and control were vested in the hands of individuals. What we understand by the concept of Italianate gardens are ancient classic themes elaborated to the ultimate degree. Their formality, symmetry and elaboration were carried back to France by Charles V. In time all this combined with the rides and allées cut through the forests of northern France to produce extensive views and vistas, thereby extending the concept of formality out into the countryside, tamed by the rules of symmetry governing the Franco/Italianate garden. It was also, of course, thereby stamping the property with the signature and individuality of ownership.

The art of France, both in horticulture and painting, had enormous influence on the English. They also made their knots and parterres, after French and Dutch models, in the seventeenth century. But when classicism became all the rage and Claude and Watteau filled their canvases with idealized landscapes, the English felt constrained to produce their own version. France was flat and England is all up hill and down dale. French formality was loosened up by William Kent, the 'father of the English landscape movement', with classic bits and pieces of temples on mounds and arcades overlooking lakes to be discovered by a brisk walk through the park land. His recreations of idealized classic landscapes, seen in the paintings of Claude *et al.*, were finally thrown together by Capability Brown in one great idyll, the 'sublime pastorale'.

The moral of this story is that if you want a garden from antiquity you should extend your house into its outside space by pergolas or columns of some sort and make sure that every vista is controlled and ends in a stop. Give it a symmetry and geometry that is not over-elaborate but that combines walks bounded by rosemary or box and uses statuary, urns or benches in proportion. If you want English Palladianism you bring the park land right up to the house, put the flower or cutting gardens at some distance away from the house or at least in a walled enclosure, and pepper your landscape with classical allusions, such as columns, balustrades and obelisks.

CLASSIC ROTUNDA

Round houses have always had their devotees. Whether the origin of the classical rotunda of Grecian temples was developed from much earlier building concepts founded in necessity – like the Celtic Neolithic settlement of a clutch of small round stone dwellings on Skara Brae in the Orkneys, which is dated to 3000 BC – or whether it reflects a primeval desire return to the womb is irrelevant. We do know that Palladio took the Temple of Vesta at Tivola as his example from ancient Rome and that from this he developed his famous Villa Rotonda theme, first at Vicenza (1567–9) and then for the Villa Foscare (La Malcontenda) on the Brenta during the sixteenth century. It was copied ecstatically in eighteenth-century Britain by Lord Burlington for his own Villa Rotonda at Chiswick, London.

It has to be said that a rotunda has its attractions: the classical recreation of a magic circle, whole and complete, the very embodiment of a Platonic idea – until that is, we recall the oh-so-solid rectilinearity of beds and wardrobes, sideboards

and cookers. Brave enough to take on the challenge, and clever enough to deflect the architectural problems, were the owners and the interior designer, David Mlinaric, who used the rotunda with its central dome as the core of the house and gave it four porticoes, each with their main rectangular rooms behind them.

In consequence the central inner hall is circular, with marble pillars and pilasters – though warmed by a modern fire, whose surround follows the lines of the Greek key pattern. The detail of the plaster cornice work is pure eighteenth century: the circular glass-topped table on a triform marble pedestal is pure twentieth century. By keeping all the colours, as well as that of the walls to those of naturally occurring stones, including marbles, the composition is all of a piece. It is presided over by

Above: The rotunda sits proudly on its knoll in true Palladian style. A ha-ha ditch runs along the base of the hillock, dividing the house from its park.

Right: This is a modern re-interpretation of the classic rotunda with exaggerated frieze- and cornice-work.

The elaborate details of the hangings, chandelier, fireplace, carpet and corner table are unified by the plain, cream-painted walls and blond floorboards, showing how modern furnishings can be integrated with reminders of classic detail.

the sculpture where sensuous female forms are realized, as in antiquity, in cold marble. This classical tension is echoed by the mix of antique and contemporary detail.

At first sight the drawing room appears wholly eighteenth-century classic. The brilliant cut chandelier is there, as is the eighteenth-century mirror over the fireplace. The cornice detail and frieze look original, the looping of drapery is in place, and the overall colour appears authentic. But look again. The sofa and side-tables are modern. Ironically, the checked back of one of the elbow chairs looks modern but is, in fact, eighteenth century.

The dining room enjoys an eighteenth-century fire surround, and over it, an ornate, gilded glass. The dining table is period as are the chairs but their upholstery, like the glass on the table is twentieth century. The room is warmed by the colour and style of eighteenth-century fabrics – apart from the chairs – and is lit by the Venetian glass chandelier, which is from the isle of Murano, famed for the tradition and style of its hand-blown glass, but which takes full advantage of twentieth-century electricity.

Upstairs an Empire-style bateau-lit, with authentic drapes and crown, is carried out in contemporary fabric, as is the curtaining to the

Pieces from a range of periods, including the canopied bateau-lit in the Empire style, are brought together against the cream-coloured wall covering and dado.

Simplified eighteenth-century-style panels and door cases, with bergère infills, are a restrained backdrop for the pride of the bathroom, the Victorian, copper and brass, state-of-the-art shower fitting.

Viewed from the rotunda, rolling English park land provides a substitute for the *compagna* of a Claudian landscape painting.

sash window. The Greek key border to the carpet is a reminder of the essential origins on which the house was conceived and its *en suite* bathroom, with bergère panels is a witty reminder of the period, especially when the cork tiling to the floor echoes the colour of the bergère panels of the walls.

It is interesting that we think of the classic garden as being something logical, formal and

proportioned, and yet the grounds that were fashioned by eighteenth-century landscapers to surround their classical buildings were anything but. The aim of the English Landscape Movement was to create an idealized rolling landscape which 'improved' on the rawness of nature by controlling the entirety of the panorama. Thus sweeping views and vistas from the house were to be made, lakes

Classic in its formality and Englishness, this formal grass walk, terminating in a seat, is, in origin, more nineteenth than eighteenth century, for the perennial borders on either side of the lawn were born of the Arts & Crafts movement, which developed as a reaction to industrialization.

were to be created within the hollows of the ground – and if there were no hollows, they would be dug – and groupings of essentially native trees – anything from a choice three to a whole stand – planted to complete the picture.

As well as the view from the house, the view to the house was also the subject of design. On its approach the landscape was manipulated into a series of classic pictures culminating in the final crescendo of the house itself. The great exponent of this style was Lancelot (Capability) Brown (1716–83), so named because he would look at a landscape and murmur 'Well, it has capabilities'. The garden surrounding this house could be said to be classic in that it follows Brown's precepts, being the culminating classic object sitting proudly on a knoll within its pastoral setting. Little attempt is made to integrate the two but that is not the point: indeed to do so would run counter to the eighteenth-century landscape ideal. As it happens, wide porticoes allow for outside use of the house –

but this usage does not impinge upon the surround.

The soft views of rich agricultural land extend all around and into the far distance, and the broad reach of water on the other side completes the tranquillity of the scene. To further the feeling of built sophistication meeting pastoral surround head-on, much of the house is surrounded by an unseen ha-ha ditch, which keeps stock grazing the park at bay.

The craft of gardening was not part of the eighteenth-century landscape philosophy. Fruit, flowers and vegetables were always grown screened, in a walled enclosure at some distance from the house. But as this is also a twentieth-century garden, it includes some fine perennial borders carried out in the grand manner of Miss Jekyll, and the long grass walk terminates in a Lutyens bench whose blue-grey paintwork is a ground level reflection of the colour of the Atlantic cedar towering behind it. All of which is equally classic in its own way.

ECCENTRIC FOLLY

When people buy historic houses and their estates with the intention of restoring them in a manner reflecting their former glory, it is often said that they do not know what they are taking on. Such doubts could never be raised in the case of the late Gervase Jackson-Stops. A distinguished architectural historian, he was architectural adviser to the National Trust and hence knew only too well the extent of his undertaking when he bought for himself the ruins of a Georgian folly and its somewhat unusual grounds in the park of Horton House, Northamptonshire. For this was no run-of-the-mill folly: it was an eighteenth-century theme park and safari park rolled into one. Where tigers once prowled, burning bright in the shadow of the eye-catcher, where Horace Walpole in 1763 found 'racoons that breed there much', a bear, and 'wart hogs with navels on their backs', Jackson-Stops created a garden of classical Georgian conceits to surround his restoration of the house, the eye-catcher itself. But if their bones are eighteenth century, the flesh is living.

The Menagerie was built by Thomas Wright of Durham in the 1750s. It was ruinous when Jackson-Stops took it on, but he restored all the fine plasterwork to the house and, most importantly, that of the saloon. All the elements of grander Palladian houses are reflected in this scaled-down version: the pilastered entrance, the elaborate cornice, egg and dart, and rope mouldings, and plaster-work medallions – here of the astrological signs of the zodiac in relief. The colours throughout the house are authentic and there are many genuine pieces of the period.

But all that did not prevent the house from being used for contemporary living, from mixing comfortable sofas and armchairs with Hepplewhite, or carved Georgian chandeliers with

Above: The preservation of architectural details, such as the mouldings to the window, is more important in the re-creation of the classic style than the presence of a bust.

Right: The Palladian pilasters, cornice and frieze, which can seem cold and formal, are warmed by the apricot wash on the walls and softened by well-worn sofas and chintz drapes.

Above: Full, elaborate drapes do not always confer formality. In this small bedroom they create a cosy effect and contrast lining prevents them looking gloomy.

Opposite: The fake marble treatment of the walls and a modern obelisk are reminders of the classical period.

electric table lamps. The saloon is based on the pale apricot paintwork to the walls. While the carpet and sofa echo this colouring and others contrast, there is no room here for twentieth-century designer rules. This is a beautiful house, beautifully restored but it is not, thank goodness, a monument to vogue.

The style of the study is timeless. The Venetian window with exposed stone reveals is the only clue to the age of the house: it is dressed with the style of swagging appropriate to the period but using the fabric of today. The skylight is a modern interpretation of earlier fancies. In this room, as in all the other rooms of the house, all the objects are proof of the attachment of their owners. There are too many over-designed houses, where the statuary, the books, the ornaments, the carpets, the furniture, are mere shadows flitting across an interior decorator's mind. The books in your house should be books that you read and use and have loved, not books that you think should be seen, or whose jackets look good with the colour-scheme.

The dining room is a deliberate mix of styles. The colour is cream and ochre; the window is pure

Georgian and the panelling of the cupboards a passing echo; the candelabrum is Georgian silver and the glass is modern.

What is clever about this house, including the fact that its architectural fabric has been superbly restored while remaining a home for real people, as all the best houses do, are the witty period touches to contemporary rooms. The bathroom enjoys Georgian colour to its walls, and the much-favoured marble paint effect below the dado rail as well, of course, as eighteenth-century maps and twentieth-century bath. The bedroom is wholly period, in curtaining and swagging, and in colour, with darker banding to the joints between walls, and between walls and ceiling.

When you come into the garden you realize how cleverly Jackson-Stops matched the restoration of the house to the creation of the garden. Not being inclined to restore the grounds to the roving wart hogs, Jackson-Stops decided to recreate all the splendours of a grand Georgian estate, with its temples, arbours, avenues, vistas, mount, ha-ha, parterre and classical allusions – in sum, all the conceits that you would expect of somewhere with the acreage of Stowe – only within a much smaller scale. If the classic twists are intriguing, the modern spin is entrancing – as we shall see. Just like the house, in fact.

One did not walk out of the great Palladian mansions into a garden, as such, one walked into a landscape. The formal, cultivated gardens were traditionally at a distance from the house. At the Menagerie, however, Jackson-Stops introduced a full herbaceous border on the south side of the house, while the north side is grassed to the entrance, the links being a double flight of steps on the one side and a columned portico on the other. The rose garden and the monkey puzzle parterre are situated at either end of the house.

From the south front of the house the green forms a large semicircle bounded by hedging. Central with the portico lies the main vista of lime avenues and hornbeam hedges, radiating in three straight lines in the goosefoot – *patte d'oie* – design

Another eccentricity of this folly was the introduction of a herbaceous border to run along its southern façade. Magnificent though it is, it is not historically accurate in terms of styling.

beloved of the period. Between these avenues are a series of serpentine paths (another stylistic device of the period) through shrubberies that lead to the various classical conceits. A third of the way down the central avenue, which gives a vista to the very

end of the garden, is the Mount, a favoured device of the eighteenth century for obtaining a viewpoint. The green path snaking around it until it reaches the top is encircled by *Acaena microphylla*, traditionally a spreading rock plant of

bronze leaflets and red spiky bracts and a brainwave for this site because the Mount was constructed of builder's rubble.

The two short avenues on each side culminate in fountains. Wright, the original architect, had left

The Tuscan arbour seen through a serpentine flower garden. The thatched, domed roof is supported by tree trunks.

plans for two circular pools. Now realized and dominated by fountains, they provide shorter focal points that balance the length of the main avenue. Behind these lie the two arbours, framed by entrances through the hedging. They are witty plays on the eighteenth century's renaissance of classicism. The Tuscan arbour is entirely rustic with walls of bark and a thatched domed roof, and the pillars for the portico are single tree trunks.

Like its companion temple on the other side, the Gothic arbour, with a Gothic stylized portico that would have done justice to Strawberry Hill, is an essay in the wits, whims and fancies of the eighteenth century. Some of the reasons they are both so amusing may be apparent only to the historian of ancient and eighteenth-century

architectures, but some of the jokes may be easily explained. The eighteenth-century estate owner was fond of making Greek temples in his grounds. He was also fond of arbours, grottoes (decorated with shells) and rustic retreats. Some even went to so far as to employ resident hermits. Just as houses and furniture enjoyed a vogue for the Gothic, so this spread to the design of summerhouses and gazebos. Jackson-Stops conflated these various fashions. All the elements of eighteenth-century passions are there, but they have been treated to an amusing twentieth-century twist.

The same has happened in the rest of the garden. Where serpentine paths would have threaded through the shrubberies and woodland, past great pools and over the rise and fall of landscapes, as

The temple, a companion to the Tuscan arbour, is in the Gothic manner. They face each other across the main axis of the garden, with a circular pool in front of each.

Another favourite eighteenth-century feature was the obelisk, which in this instance was placed on a grassy mound with a spiral path.

they did and do at Rousham, one of the best of William Kent's designs, serpentine paths at the Menagerie wend through soft informal planting, clumps of white geraniums and sprays of pink and white roses, backed by towers of yellow lupins and dark pink hollyhocks.

This soft liveable-in-ness of Jackson-Stops' treatment of the garden is what makes it contemporary. The formal edging to the beds of low box is all left behind; the rose garden is threaded with sweet rocket and waving foxgloves; the grass verges to the Vernal or Spring Garden are populated by ragged robin, not tight little rows of grape hyacinth.

Just as the eighteenth-century structure of the house has been restored, giving the living in it over to real people in favourite armchairs not set period pieces, so the structure of an eighteenth-century garden has been created, dressed in the less informal and more ecologically attuned attire of modern times.

NEO-CLASSICAL PORTUGUESE VILLA

This remarkable neo-classical house sits on a hilltop in Portugal overlooking the broad wash of the Atlantic. Somewhere in its ancestry lurks Palladio's Villa Rotonda, although its arid setting puts it nearer ancient Greece than the fertile blue-green valleys of Italy. Bold and solid, it is designed by David Hicks with an eye to fine detail. A meticulous transition from house to garden is made through the four porticoes, which take you outside to in, and inside to out.

The entrance portico is magnificent in its simplicity, with four white Doric columns offset by walls faced with a concrete mixed from local sand, stone and terracotta particles. This is an impressive entrance by any standard, guarded by two carved supercilious dogs.

Progressing into the house, one enters the hall,

large enough to double as another dining room, seating twenty. The geometric lozenges used for the ground were designed by David Hicks in a combination of stone, wood and glazed terracotta. The colour of the walls takes its cue from the stone of the ground so the transition is less perceptible. There are two striking features about this room. The first is the floor; the second is the use of chunks of neo-classic detail, made the more striking because they are discontinuous, as if they were broken-off relics that had been culled from an

Above: The splendid rear façade of the house is reflected in its swimming pool, which, in turn, picks up the azure of the sea beyond.

Right: The door case, brilliant against slate blue walls, is a stylish simplification of classical detail, a theme also picked up by the generously sized balusters and splats.

archaeological expedition. They are, in fact, a post-modernist treatment of an ancient theme.

In the *sala*, or big room, this post-modernist effect playing with ancient themes is even more evident. At one end is an early eighteenth-century English chimney piece, a classical marble piece, surmounted by a modern glass and broken pediment. At the other end of the room, are three rectangular glazed openings – two are windows, the central one is a double door – and above each is a large porthole. These rectangles might be entrances to some Egyptian dynastic tomb: in fact they give on to the swimming pool. This is a room for eclecticism: contemporary abstract landscapes, eighteenth-century England, circular side-tables draped in the Victorian manner but using local modern cloth, neo-classic console tables in blond sycamore, and late eighteenth-century Portuguese pots, a Brussels weave carpet echoing Persian designs, all against a background of artist's canvas stretched over the wall.

The dining room departs from the eclectic bustle of the *sala* in its restoration of eighteenth-century England, recollected in the tranquillity of green walls, authentic chimney piece, architectural engravings, splat-back, neo-Chippendale dining chairs, Staffordshire pottery and a view of Venice from the Basilica San Marco. In total contrast is the other room off the *sala*, the card room, in walls of outrageous pink, furnished with 200 black and white engravings, with an Egyptian revival fire-place and neo-Egyptian triangular bookcases to Hicks' own design.

Hotter countries and stronger light allow for the use of bolder colour both inside and out. Upstairs the principal bedroom suite has used a kilometre of apricot cotton to be stretched in loose pleats around its walls. It bears close scrutiny for there are intriguing historical evocations. Classical Wedgwood plaques to the English white marble fireplace, certainly, but there are hints of earlier historical periods, too. A latticed armoire has a battlemented pediment, and the corona above the bed hints of medieval pennants.

At the far end of the *sala* the door and windows, which open onto the swimming pool, are symbolic of a variety of architectural styles, from ancient Egyptian to Classical and Modernist. The house has been carefully designed to take account of its situation, and the statue visible through the door has been positioned to draw the eye across the pool to the landscape beyond.

Right: In contrast to the *sala*, the dining room is classic eighteenth-century English in style, both in architectural detail and furnishings.

Opposite above: The journey through the house traverses several architectural epochs, all linked by the modern treatment of its historical themes. The medieval cut of the corona above the bed contrasts sharply with the pleated silk of the walls, but the general effect conjures up visions of royal tents at jousts.

Opposite below: The card room sustains the eighteenth-century theme, despite the Perspex tables.

The exterior exhibits a stunning simplicity. The loggia portico overlooking the swimming pool is perhaps the most spectacular feature and shows that contemporary usage does not detract from a classic concept. The pool surround, of stone and brick, blends beautifully with the house. From the house, across the pool, a piece of white statuary is backed by a dark *Pinus pinea* (umbrella pine). Beyond is the blue Atlantic, blending the colours of sea and pool and sky in a spectrum of azure. The composition is not classical, in that the components are not symmetrically balanced, but the components are classical and a modern balance is achieved.

The use of statuary – sculptures and urns – is appropriate to the scale and flavour of the house – big, bold and uncompromising. Planting up the urns would soften them – the intention is to retain their sculptural lines unimpeded. The stained dark green treillage (lattice fencing) is part of the scheme of grand-scale classic – a *tour de force*.

Right: The view from the rear portico is simply stunning. Greek in its white-heat simplicity, yet softened by the pink of terracotta tile work. Here is a lesson in asymmetry: the trunks of the off-centre pine are repeated in the statuary legs and then in the columns, while the dark pine provides the backdrop.

Left: David Hicks uses urns as if they were statuary. Planting would weaken their dramatic, stark effect.

COUNTRY STYLE

The concept of a country house and garden is an ideal. In the imagination it is invariably old, which is odd, because there are a great many modern houses in the country; it is probably English (historically, the seat of power lay in the country), yet Kansas and New Zealand and Barbados have their share of country houses; it is light and airy, which does not necessarily follow at all; it is filled with flowers, red Turkey rugs and dogs, none of which are the monopoly of country houses. In the mind's eye it will have a large garden, with wide herbaceous borders stocked with dark blue delphiniums and deep red peonies, sweet-scented roses (of the old-fashioned variety) will climb the length and breadth of old brick or stone walls (there is hardly a panel fence to be seen in the mind's eye), and the walled kitchen garden will be bursting with perfect fruits (with never an aphid to be seen).

Perhaps we fondly believe that although country houses are not all like that now, that is how they used to be. Well, we would be wrong. When James Lees-Milne was secretary to the Country Houses Committee of the National Trust, he went about Britain, evaluating houses for acquisition by the Trust. It was the last years of the Second World War. Many owners were without heirs, having lost their sons in action; many others were impoverished and their heirs were faced with exorbitant inheritance taxes. Recent changes in the law had enabled them to make over property to the Trust in lieu of taxes, and the purpose of Lees-Milne's travels was to inspect those properties that might be suitable for such an arrangement.

Among the houses that Lees-Milne visited was Nether Lypiatt Manor, near Stroud, Gloucestershire. It was an unspoilt late seventeenth-century house:

> perfect in every way. In fact, an ideal, if not the ideal small country house. It retains all the wainscoting, doors with high brass handles and locks, one lovely chimney piece in the hall, of white stone against a ground of blue slate. The rich staircase has three twisted balusters to each tread.

Luncheon, however, 'consisted of one egg in a jacketed potato'.

If Nether Lypiatt was ideal, the Moat House, Warwickshire, was 'an archaeologist's gem'. A yeoman's house, built in 1480, it had been owned by the Misses Smythe's family since 1743. It was also 'wonderfully uncomfortable. There is no telephone, no water – but a pump in the garden – no heating, no light, no bath and no water closet – but an outdoor twin earth closet also in the garden'.

At the other end of the country house spectrum was the Victorian Eaton Hall (since razed and rebuilt), seat of the Duke of Westminster and never offered to the National Trust. 'Eaton was more like a town than a house ... [it] could house 100 guests, each with a servant and still there was room for more.'

If we attempt to elicit those elements that connote the country garden we arrive at, ultimately, a bit of this and a bit of that. In most cases scale is a factor – country gardens are usually larger than urban spaces. Some of the layout perhaps, such as the knot parterre edged in low box, will echo or even have its origins in the seventeenth-century house for which it was made. The rest of it may correspond to the whims of successive owners, culminating in the glory of the late nineteenth-century country garden, which has come to personify its archetype. At the heart of the country garden, whatever it is, are plants – adorning a wall, overflowing from pots, marking a doorway or creating shade. Borders, rather than small flower beds, are common, simply because of the available space, and

Above right: Outhouses were an essential part of country living – for the animals, for storage and for tools. The dovecote, too, usually found a place, although it was not then a decorative feature but provided food for the table.

Below right: The simplicity, comfort and informality of this room illustrate one aspect of country style. Decoration in the form of pictures, flowers and a painted cupboard is appropriately unobtrusive.

many country gardens include a vegetable patch and fruit garden.

Edwin Lutyens and Gertrude Jekyll will be remembered as the chief exponents of this apogee of country gardening, from the end of the nineteenth century until the First World War, even though there were many other gardeners who had practised the country garden look long before them, as, for example, at Arley Hall, Cheshire.

When it was newly completed, the Lutyens–Jekyll look was far more structured than we see in nostalgic hindsight. The years between then and now have mellowed these gardens – age has matured, rather than withered them, and it is this mellowing combined with the inclusive references to earlier styles that defines the country garden more than anything else. It is a sophisticated assortment of idioms overlaid with the patina of age and maturity.

A town garden needs a much crisper look, simply because its size alone precludes ramble. The cottage garden must, of course, be strictly managed, for although it may look like a carefree jumble, it requires more effort than any other style to keep it like that. Most modern gardens have not had time to mellow, and classic gardens are too precise, even though in neglect they offer more charms of nostalgia and ruin than any other.

The terrace is a vital part of the country garden. The hard, clean surface services the transition between inside and out, for eating and entertainment and the coming and going of bare feet in summer and muddy boots and overshoes in winter. It can be sited to catch a view or the sun or to avoid the sun or a draught, and it is bound up with doors and windows, recesses and protuberances, pergolas and overhangs, walls and steps. All this must be in tune with the building, styled to harmonize with the interior and yet be functional for the family that uses it. An expanse of lawn is a prerequisite, and a tennis court or swimming pool can be added if there is space and the determination. Many suburban gardens are large enough to be styled in this way.

A country garden need not, of course, be necessarily constructed according to the precepts of Gertrude Jekyll and her supporters. A Californian or Australian will think of a country garden in a different way. Grow a field of lavender and live in Provence. Choose cypress, an oil jar and a vine and be in Italy. The permutations of Californian, Southwestern and Moorish are all available; each has an ethnic styling overlay that can be defined in hard surfacing, furnishing and planting.

The general looseness of definition of both the country house and its garden makes it impossible to lay down strict rules for its style of decoration or its style of garden. If you take on a period house, you are not compelled to keep it in the style for which it was designed. After all, a contemporary style is merely the last in a succession of changes. If you keep to the period in which the house was built, do you merely conserve it by preserving what there is or restore it? Many houses, if merely conserved, would be uninhabitable by modern standards. If you restore a house with a long history, what date do you take as its reference point? When it was built? Its Georgian heyday? Do you demolish the wing that was a Victorian addition? When Uppark House, West Sussex, was destroyed by fire, the National Trust had to decide whether to restore it as it had been in 1690 when it had been built or to re-create it as it was when the Trust acquired it, including the extensive alterations that had been made at the end of the eighteenth century. They opted for the latter.

The only rule that makes any sense for styling country houses and their gardens is that, regardless of size or date, they should respond appropriately to their setting. Be considerate of the interface between the garden and the surrounding land. Nearer the house the garden can be more formal, but as it moves towards fields or mountains or rivers it needs to take on a more natural look, or the juncture will be too abrupt. A garden in the classical style balances urns on either side of the doorway; the country garden can use clumps of rosemary. It would be as inappropriate to create a mini-Versailles around a Scottish stone manse as it would be to replace the doors and their high brass handles at Nether Lypiatt with elaborately panelled and moulded doors in the style of Louis XIV. It is all about respect.

Chintz and white paintwork have come to epitomize the country look. Not all country houses have such a light and airy quality to their halls as here, where the double glass doors make it possible for the outer doors to be left open, bringing the outside in.

Despite the stencilling, this is an austere treatment for a bedroom, although a traditional feel is introduced by the solid wooden bed and the floral curtains.

HUNTING LODGE

Once upon a time, runs the lore and legend of Hampshire, there was a royal hunting lodge in the vicinity of the Manor of Dogmersfield. No one is quite sure to whom the hunting lodge belonged – King John, perhaps, who built Odiham Castle nearby, or Henry VII, who accompanied his son Prince Arthur to his first meeting with his bride-to-be Catherine of Aragon at Dogmersfield on her way from Portsmouth to London – but that is immaterial, for historically half of Hampshire was convinced that this small eighteenth-century house, built in Jacobean style, was a royal Tudor hunting lodge.

Such is the stuff of myths. All the evidence, in fact, suggests that this extraordinary building was the last remnant of a series of follies designed for

Above: A rustic lad in stone, set off by hornbeam, is a wonderful foil to the ogee-type façade of the house beyond.

Right: The extraordinary brick façade of the house provides a theatrical backdrop to the garden. A straight mown path through hornbeam hedges links the house to the lake.

An easy informality and elegance without affectation are wholly appropriate to a period country house, achieved here with a plain, plump sofa, cushions, pictures and flowers.

one Paulet St John, who, in the 1740s, set about an elaborate rococo creation for the grounds of what had become Dogmersfield Park. There was a Belvedere (a miniature fort with mock battlements), a Palladian bridge and a Gothic arch floating like a solid tiara on the hilltop. All, except for the 'hunting lodge', which was tucked away in the woods, were swept away some fifty years later in the name of 'improvement' under the hand of Eames, a pupil of Capability Brown.

Whether it was originally a hunting lodge, or whether it was only a keeper's cottage or possibly a fishing pavilion – it sits only about 90 metres (100 yards) from the lake – we shall never know. There is nothing about the house itself to suggest that it is pre-eighteenth century, and it is so much in the style of the Gothic arch, of which only pictures remain, that we must conclude that it was at least given its extraordinary façade to enliven the view from the Belvedere in the 1740s. Like the arch, it was originally rendered and whitewashed, with the gables and window mouldings picked out in red. It must have looked quite extraordinary.

In 1947 the house was bought by the celebrated

decorator, the late John Fowler, and he gave the interior a formal elegance, installing the carved eighteenth-century chimney piece and his own delicate period furniture. There was no garden to speak of when he acquired the property, and he laid out a garden of exquisite formality, with clipped Portugal laurels and pleached hornbeams to frame the façade on one side and the view of the lake on the other. He bequeathed the property to the National Trust, which leases it to the interior designer and architect Nicholas Haslam who, while he admires Fowler's work, has nevertheless allowed a more relaxed, late twentieth-century approach to predominate.

In consequence, some of the more artificial aspects of Fowler's decoration have been replaced by equally civilized but less formal schemes. The drawing room is simply rough-brushed in muted terracotta tints, which pick up those of the collection of drawings, and elaboration has been replaced by a modern sofa, of elegant shape but plump and loose-covered in white. Unadorned terracotta pots filled with pale pink and sugar pink flowers give a pretty but unaffected lift to the colours of the room, and plenty of books and cushions make for an overall sense of relaxation.

The study has the same feel, but more so. Here the terracotta washes not only the walls and ceiling but also the door frames and doors and the timber supporting posts and beams. Mixed with old red rugs, a lime-coloured throw over a lumpy old sofa and a fringed terracotta throw over the table, are a bergère library chair and an oak kneehole desk. Pictures, books, cushions, a mix of fabrics and patterns and colours are all brought together by the warmth of the predominant terracotta to make this room natural and unpretentious, as inviting for a drink and a chat as for whole days reading and writing. Just as the other room is a country drawing room, so this is very much a country study.

The long quarry-tiled hall has not been smartened up into something it is not. The paint peels quietly off the walls, the leather chairs and settee are well worn and the baskets for logs and twigs

Above: Terracotta has been used in the study not only for the walls and ceiling but also for the lintels and beams to introduce a unifying element into what might otherwise become fractured lines.

Left: The timber-boarded passage leading to the kitchen has been painted a cheerful yellow and decorated with an array of baskets.

are unhidden. The kitchen has not been modernized either. While some would have been tempted to do a 'farmhouse' with limed oak 'units' and curly cut-outs, Nicholas Haslam has left most of it alone. The stainless steels sinks and drainer and the unassuming, cream-painted cupboards are

Above: The way from the garden to the lake is through white gothic timber gates.

Left: Statuary can seem superfluous, but this hunter and his dog seem entirely appropriate.

practical. The lighting has been improved with reflectors set into the ceiling, but they are not obtrusive. The attention in the kitchen is focused on the light from the window and the simple, open shelves, whose practical pots and bowls are decoration enough. The timber-boarded passage outside the kitchen has been jollified with sunshine yellow paint and a variety of baskets.

The house faces south and looks over to the lake.

It sits easily in its pastoral landscape with, on one side, views over the surrounding park land and, on the other, pavilions, arbours, nooks and crannies. The lines of the house created by doors and windows do not work directly with the garden layout, but house and garden are linked by greenery and garden furniture.

All the formal green bones of the garden have been retained as Fowler made it. The wide green

Above: Garden rooms look into small, formal, box-edged gardens that are punctuated by box pyramids.

Opposite: This very beautiful gothic garden pavilion was designed by John Fowler as one of a pair.

everywhere, and partly because the façade of the house is so elaborate in itself that it needs the sculptured greenery to balance it.

On the cross-axes Fowler constructed two Gothic pavilions of great charm, the shape of whose latticed entrances echo the ogee gables of the façade of the house. Off the main axis Fowler built a series of garden rooms, with straight gravel paths and deep borders punctuated by small box pyramids. At the end of the garden a cruciform gravel path is delineated by dwarf box hedging. These terminate in his garden room, which looks to the garden on one side and the lake and woods on the other.

The planting has become a little looser than it was in Fowler's time. Foxgloves have been allowed to seed themselves among pink roses and white marguerites, and bushes of rosemary are allowed to grow fat, squeezed between the box shapes. Some of the borders are no longer

lawn in front of the house is still surrounded on all three sides by the high hedges of pleached horn-beam, with a gap in the hedge facing the house and a pair of white gates beyond, which open to give a vista directly out from the house, across the green and over to the lake. The clipped domes of the Portuguese laurels still stand at the break in the hedge – the overall effect is formal and architectural, certainly, but it is not overly elaborate, partly because of the entirety of green

as neat or as deep or as luxuriantly planted as they once were, but this gives the garden its country touch. It is in keeping with the easy informality inside the house and the natural magnificence of the surrounding woods and waters.

Some gardens look lived in, and this is such a one. It is like an expensive coat that has been well worn – style shows through. Time, of course, mellows even the most extreme designs, softening its edges, but its proportions still work.

PROVENÇAL RETREAT

Provence is one of France's national treasures. A *département* that brings with it inland seas of lavender and pots of honey, the mysteries and money of the perfume industry, and at its shores the warm and tideless waters of the Mediterranean with its own fruits of the sea – the warm and wealthy bodies of its tourists and habitués that can only fire the ardour of national pride that beats in every Frenchman's breast.

Provence bears comparison with Tuscany, the setting for the conversion of an old farm cottage described in the next chapter. Olives and vines were and are staples, and both were included in the itinerary for the Grand Tour. Although Tuscany won its pilgrims earlier, Provence won them later and more enduringly: the *beau monde*

have made camp here ever since. The climate is kinder in Provence: there is more rainfall, the land is richer and lusher, the summers are not as hot, the winters are not as cold. The English have longer repaired to coastal Provence, building British gardens with artistry and style, taking advantage of climate and soil and the natural vegetation – the maquis or garigue which they have now re-imported as garden plants: the cistus, genista, arbutus and the common herbs such as rosemary and lavender. It is the combination of social history, climate, soil and systems of land tenure that have made the south of France ideal for a more *soigné* sort of country living than Tuscany enjoyed. Of course Tuscany did, and does, to a certain extent, but not as much.

This house sits on a hill among a cluster of other houses. Inside it is pink and white with touches of green. Each room is treated with an appropriate degree of sophistication. The salon has a plastered ceiling, and the beams have been plastered over also. A chandelier, white loose covers for the sofa

Above: A place for relaxation is what Provence is all about. This early bamboo reclining chair is very tempting. The patina of the wall colour takes many years to build up.

Left: Salmon and white, for both soft furnishings and paintwork, is a light, elegant and very French. Quarry tiles establish the room's country location.

The overall shape of the kitchen has probably altered little over the years. The smart ovens are given the country treatment by the use of small-patterned tiles and dragged paintwork on the cupboard doors.

and armchairs, and white or pale green-brushed paintwork to the tables give this room an elegance. The walls are banded and panelled in salmon pink on white, but these are all paint effects rather than plaster or woodwork.

The dining room is more traditional French in flavour. The open top half of the pale green cupboard doors, their pleated fabric lining, and the curves and panelling to the doors are typically French, as is the china on the shelves. But the rough dark salmon brushwork to the timber boards is a repeat of the treatment to the boards of the ceiling, the painted chairs and the chandelier, together with

Right: The staircase repeats the pink, salmon and green shades found elsewhere in the house, and the minimal decoration is in keeping with the country atmosphere.

Far right: All lined up and ready for the sun: deck chairs, spaced out between citrus in traditional terracotta pots. Note the terracotta uplighters at the base of each pot for night-time effect.

Left: To unify the dining end of the kitchen with the cooking end, chairs and table are dressed in patterned Provençal fabrics. In a clever continuity of themes, the deep salmon shades reflect those found elsewhere in the house.

cotton Provençal fabrics, are moving towards a less sophisticated and more countrified look.

In fact, the dining room is the other end of the kitchen, which repeats the same pale green panelling to its cupboard doors and the shutters to the windows, and uses tiles of a more vivid green in smaller and larger patterns to surround state-of-the-art ovens and hob. This kitchen would have been utterly spoilt by festooning its circumference with built-in furniture and cupboards. It uses a free-standing old butcher's table and odd shelves, which are very much more in keeping with Provençal farmhouse kitchens. It adds an air of grandeur with an occasional painting, but in essence, and despite the up-to-date machinery, it does not stray from the old French feel.

The bedroom uses the same approach. Bed-hangings about the simple lines of an iron four-poster are country checks and Provençal sprigs, repeated in plain pleated curtains. The rest of the room uses white-painted furniture against simple white walls.

There are two staircases to this house. There is the interior staircase and an exterior one. Where

possible, the colours used inside the house are repeated outside – the exterior staircase is dark salmon pink up to the upstairs balcony, but is set against a sugar-pink wall, banded in white at the entrance through pale green doors. This juxtaposition of colours, which repeats inside themes outside, and includes the tiling to the steps, makes for a frisson of recognition of the already known and the newly encountered.

As the living moves outside, the residual exterior walling continues in dark salmon pink, offset by the sugar pink flowerheads of hydrangea. At the back of the house the combinations of native Provence, country living and formality come together in strong architectural lines mixed with native planting. The rectangular swimming pool is set at a diamond angle to the house, and the two urns at its furthest end provide a focal point beyond the pool itself. The formal triangle hedged with lavender surrounding a pollarded olive tree, which lies between the house and the pool, follows the line of the pool but softens it by using planting. A stone edging instead of lavender would have made the overall design too formal, too

Opposite: The colour and type of the roof tiles, the texture of the walls, the green of the shutters and the olive-grey foliage are unmistakably Provençal. Add the clipped lavender and massed geraniums with the wicker chairs to complete the effect. The positioning of the plunge pool on the diagonal adds further interest.

artificial. As it is, the overall design provides length and elegance and at the same time links the country house with pool and setting.

The walls around the other side of the house are simply stone. In keeping with this, the vine-draped pergola, bench and table are of grey-painted timber, and the blue-grey of the shutters picks up the blue-grey of the foliage of the clumps of anthemis, with their white stars, in the ground beneath. The path to the back gate, a fairly impressive structure adorned by pineapples and black-painted wrought iron, has a deep border to one side, in which swathes of anthemis again are interwoven with local lavender, the whole given a

Above: The small front garden looks out over surrounding villas, the tall Mediterranean cypress framing the view.

more formal interpretation by symmetrically placed balls of box, standard trees and pencil cypresses.

Behind the house the garden begins to run into the land, and the stone shelter, now used to house garden equipment, is the beginning of the end of formality and a start to the return of husbandry.

COUNTRY ESTATE

This is a grand treatment of a country house in Oxfordshire, designed, inside and out, by David Hicks. Originally a small farmhouse of the early eighteenth century, a double-height drawing room was added in 1825. It now has six bedrooms and five bathrooms. Two columns, removed from a Regency shop-front, and the lintel above them were added to the façade, an octafoil window was installed in what used to be the loft and was converted to a bedroom, and a trellised porch was added, in keeping with the new, Gothic, half-glazed front door.

In order to create a sense of space and to give the house 'a fairly big backbone', David Hicks demolished two walls to make a long, wide, stone-flagged hall. Because the walls of this old farmhouse were uneven and did not have, nor would have had, the architectural detail of elaborate plaster work for the cornices, for example, Hicks gave them definition by banding all the edges and junctures in mid-brown offset by a plain stippled paper in pale yellow. The

balustrading to the staircase is exceptionally good and echoes the trellis work of the front door and the porch.

The drawing room was given a fully formal treatment. The walls covered in stretched rose-pink cotton match the lavishly swagged and frilled curtains. The carpet was especially woven to Hicks' design, a closely repeated geometric pattern in ivory and browns echoing the lighter shades of these colours in the raw slub silk upholstery for one of the modern sofas. The fire surround was also especially designed by Hicks. Made of ash, it includes panelling of white formica and incorporates a nineteenth-century relief marble panel. Above the fireplace hangs a long, plain mirror framed in dark green and gilded wood.

Above: The view to the north side of the house is contained by hornbeam hedges. The fence detailing is superb, with the gatepost pyramids repeated on flanking wall piers.

Left: The stone-flagged floor places the hall immediately in the country. The light and simple chairs and tables allow all the attention to be focused on the paintings.

Top: The sophisticated decor of the drawing room appears to be traditional but is in fact achieved with some very modern materials, showing that elegant country style should not be equated only with the antique.

Above: Plain, black-painted, modern bookcases blend beautifully with an old Turkey rug, a wing chair and all the other accoutrements of country style.

Beside it sits a modern sofa upholstered in bright yellow quilting.

The library's walls are entirely shelved. It is a quiet, serious, warm and comfortable room, in which the Turkey rug in its traditional bright red and dark blue has found its home. The plain brick fireplace has been left as found except for the addition of a plain marble surround, its simplicity and straight lines in keeping with the straightforward, unfussy nature and purpose of the room. The wing chair is upholstered in a contrast pale mustard and echoing black check, and the cat is upholstered in black and darker mustard tones, offset by the clean white nose and paws. Notice how the white whiskers are matched to the slash of white to the lower cheek.

The dining room has a very fresh and very French look, conveyed by the delicacy of the chairs and the mix of ivory and shades of turquoise. In fact, the chairs are copies of a late eighteenth-century English chair, the lattice back echoing the other Gothic touches to the house. They are upholstered in lighter shades of the colours used on the panelling that forms the dominant feature of the room. This is a mural, executed *en grisaille* with silver and turquoise for the owners' previous house. The wish to use this for the dining room of their new house, as opposed to say, the drawing room, meant that the structure of the dining room had to be remodelled. The room originally had a low-beamed ceiling, which would have been inappropriate for the sophisticated mural, so the floor was dug out to give the room height. The dining table is merely plywood, covered in a Hicks print. 'I can't see the point of spending a lot of money on a table and then covering it up with a tablecloth', he says. 'And I happen to like tablecloths.'

The dressing room to the bedroom for the master of the house combines library with dressing room and bathroom, with bookshelves fitted under the wash basin and over and beside the window. A nineteenth-century chintz on a black ground uses autumn browns and dull golds, colours repeated in

The charming turquoise and silver mural gives the dining room a theatrical feeling, while the delicate lattice-backed chairs are light and pretty.

the upholstery and cushions for the chairs. It is a novel, comfortable, useful and, indeed, instructive treatment for any dressing room.

One of the most satisfying tasks for any designer is to be given the opportunity to design both the house and the garden. In this case, the job was even more delightful as it involved designing the

garden from scratch. Hicks has long been exercised by the problems of the English climate, the summer being so short and 'the long, bare winter months so dreary'. His solution is an architectural garden with lines of trees that look 'pleasing all through the year and ... even more wonderful covered in snow'.

Right: This is the major view into the surrounding countryside, layered in a series of green rooms. In the foreground is the pool room, contained by horse chestnut; beyond, a chestnut avenue is reinforced by contrasting grass lengths. The final ride up the hill is terminated by a silhouette of trees.

Left: The view from the house up to the entrance gate. Statuary punctuates the angled and pleached hornbeam hedges.

The garden surrounds the house and has been designed in a series of green rooms. There is a vista from the house with a chestnut avenue, which turns into two formal flanks to the swimming pool. The swimming pool is painted black because 'if you had normal swimming pool colour, it would be impossible to have it outside the dining room, but, as it is black, it looks just like a piece of water – like a pond'. The vista from the house thus encompasses the swimming pool, without looking in the least bit out of place in Oxfordshire, runs through the avenue and over a field, almost to the horizon. It is a huge and interesting concept, making a virtue of the swimming pool, a feature notoriously difficult to integrate.

The views from the house, then, are of landscape, trees and water. The flowers are kept for the walled gardens, which are also geometrically designed. 'When it comes to design, I'm a straight line wallah who likes a formal grid (Renaissance, Gothic even Medieval)', says Hicks. 'I plant it up romantically so by September the backbone's engulfed by flowers. The plants die down and in winter you've got a bare bone structure, like this, to marvel at'.

The bones and proportions of David Hicks' concepts are their strength, for the control of space is what makes his designs work. He then overlays

A remarkable wall plaque and water feature, framed in flint. Hostas are grown in terracotta pots (so that slugs can be controlled more easily) to frame the feature.

this sound basis with decorative detail. Too often we only see the decorative bit, without understanding its vital underlying strengths. So often much of what is written and photographed in gardens is to do with decorative horticulture, omitting any explanation or appreciation of the basic structure.

The outside rooms are strongly directional. Adjacent to the house they are hedged or walled; as they move outwards, the formal allée is pleached, a tunnel created from natural materials directs the gaze into the countryside beyond, and

there are avenues of chestnut, all reinforced by differing lengths of grass, emphasized by stripes or a contrast of the rough with the mown, and, in the rough, there is a native flower meadow. This garden, as Hicks points out, 'is still a young, new garden which needs a good ten years to mature'. The techniques used here have been used in one way or another throughout garden history, but he brings them together in an exciting and truly twentieth-century mélange. This garden will be even more exciting in ten years, but by then it will be a garden of the twenty-first century.

Right and far right: To the south of the house there is a series of walled and tunnelled spaces, leading the visitor on to a final window to the outside wall.

David Hicks is a master at re-interpreting the formal idea. In his flower garden the layout is just as strict, although the soft infill of poppies, foxgloves and old roses disguises the effect through early summer. In winter the satisfactory geometry of the layout is restored.

AMERICAN CLAPBOARD HOUSE

Above: The house viewed from the garden.

Left: A pergola/porch in colonial style extends this clapboard house into its garden surround. The floor is of blue slate, and the timber roof is detailed to feel pitched from beneath, even though it is, in fact, perfectly flat, which makes an attractive additional feature to the garden façade of the house. The porch surround and the table create a pleasing unity of design.

This is one of the wittiest interpretations of the country house we have seen. A wood shingled house, typical of the northern parts of the United States, and with a traditional porch and the almost statutory swimming pool, it sits among the remaining hickory and pine trees from a cleared woodland. So far, so typical. Yet in its treatment of the interior, of the transition between house and garden, and of the garden including the pool, it constitutes an amusing commentary on three themes – classical, colonial and modern – which for their effect, needed to come together in the country.

Apart from the ruched pink silk panels, the dining room is all white – table, chairs, floor, doors, ceiling and all the panelling below the dado. The detail to the cornice, albeit in a modern, stylized interpretation, the door cases, the pediments over the windows, the fluted architraves and even the fluted pillars that form the table legs are reminiscent of classical temples, and they represent here both classical architecture and

The bright white emphasizes this modern interpretation of the classical lines of the alcove, cornice, table and chairs.

Although the emphasis is on comfort, white is again used to highlight the architectural and classical features – the column-like legs of the tables, the panelled dado and the cornice.

Limed timber boarding is a highly appropriate natural material for the converted loft of a country house. It rarely gives the same effect as fabric tenting or lining the walls with pleated silk (as in the dining room, opposite), but here it does just that.

colonial architecture. The latter, of course, was ultimately derived from the former. When the building of temples in the grounds of great country houses and the country houses themselves imitated the art of Palladio in eighteenth-century England, the fashion crossed the Atlantic, slowly but inevitably.

This reiteration of those influences has been adapted for this modern country house, cleverly avoiding all the pitfalls it could have encountered. Far from being pretentious, the result is very simple and plain, an effect helped by the lack of fussy curtaining and by the big, bold detail to the cornice. Elaborate ornamentation and decoration would have been quite wrong. The severity of the classical line does not feel at odds with modern furniture and flooring. In fact it works very well, partly because all the lines are clean and straight and partly because the use of white unifies the simple ladder-back chairs with their white-painted rush seats, the square, fluted pillars of the table

legs and the Georgian paned French windows. It is the restraint evident in the manipulation of the themes that makes it so successful.

The repetition of these themes is carried through to the drawing room. The architectural detail of cornice, panelling below the dado and fluted pilasters forming the entrance to the conservatory end of the room and, again, fluted square pillars are repeated in the legs of the coffee table. There has been a change in the use of the colour. The dining room allowed the limited use of pink; the drawing room has moved to the limited use of pale lemon for the walls, picked up in a stronger tone for the armchair. The minimal use of pattern is repeated too. In the dining room the silk was pink striped; here the stripe is a subdued green for the sofa. The use of a number of rugs gives the room a rather traditional, country feel.

The loft has been ingeniously converted. It, too, has a unified look, using hints of the classic in a modern interpretation. Green-painted floorboards

The pergola/porch, which looks into the garden, has a central entrance, moving the axes over and down the garden, but away from the asymmetric positioning of the garden door.

Right: Classic columns are used to blend a formal styling with a colonial one. This porch extension is on an axis with the swimming pool area.

and limed timber boarding cover roof and walls, fitting shelves and cupboards around the central supporting timber. All the finishing touches are there, fluted architraves and even a pediment incorporated in the roof structure.

The basic language of this house and its land is country, but the idiom is modern classic. It carries through to the garden, which is unfussy and natural. It is also a garden for family use, heavily punctuated with seating places, with arbours and pool houses, but divided from the front entrance to the house by a high yew hedge. Where there are buildings, they are carried out in the same idiom as the house.

In spring the front approach is a sea of narcissi beneath the bare trees. From the house they can be looked down upon from a first- floor deck, which in summer is the cool side of the house. Leading off one side of the house is a white-painted decked porch. Fluted classic columns in timber repeat those found inside the house, but here they are used to support the cross beams of the pergola. Such an arrangement provides an ideal outpost of the house within the garden itself. The ground is of blue slate, which gives a more contemporary feel than weathered timber boarding would.

The same classical idiom is used to create both an entrance to, and a focal point for, the

rectangular swimming pool, which is at a distance from the house. It is a pretty idea and one that both punctuates the garden and provides some useful shade in summer. In addition, it enables a translation to the outside of themes used inside the house itself – the entrance to a contemporary temple. Note the use of grass for the steps under the temple entrance, which preserves a unity with the expanse of surrounding grass. If you intend to adapt this idea for your own garden be warned: they can be tricky beyond endurance when it comes to mowing. Standard mop-head trees line either side of the pool, extending the classic feel of an arbour. The surrounding fencing is a legal requirement in the United States and must conform to a certain height for safety reasons.

This is the sort of country house and garden that works equally well as a permanent residence or as a weekend and holiday retreat. It is not overly furnished, requiring a mass of objects to be put away or furniture covered up when people are away. Its surfaces inside and out are straightforward, they can be cleaned, dusted and swept in one go. Apart from mowing, garden maintenance is minimal, for there are no vast borders to be dug and double-dug, and planted and weeded; there are no overhanging trees or vines to shed leaves on the terrace and lend a dilapidated air, advertising the fact that the place is unoccupied. When everyone returns, family and friends – for this is ideal for entertaining – life can be taken up where it was left off.

The swimming pool is approached up grass steps (difficult to mow), which lead to a classic arbour overlooking the activity. The classic motif is then repeated beyond the pool, though diminishing towards the boundary of the garden. This is a very witty reinterpretation of classic formality in modern terms, providing a feature in the general layout of the garden, a gateway to the hedged pool 'room' and a considerable area of shaded sitting space.

MANOR HOUSE

This soft stone-built house in East Sussex, with its tall Tudor chimneys and brick oast-houses, was built in 1634 by a local iron-master, and it was the home of Rudyard Kipling between 1902 and 1936, when it was acquired by the National Trust. The watermill at the bottom of the garden still grinds corn for flour and beside it is one of the world's oldest working water-driven turbines, which Kipling installed to generate electricity for the house.

Both the house and the gardens have been kept as they were in Kipling's time, but apart from the odd Tiffany lamp and the central-heating radiators there is nothing about it that would have been out of place a hundred, two hundred years ago. By the same token – and this is why we have included it in this book – there is nothing about it that would

Above: The rich oak panelling, oak floorboards and comfortable wing chair make the parlour a warm and welcoming room.

Right: This is a wonderful example of basic garden design, where the mass of the old house is extended outwards in hedging, with another linear form in the line of lime trees (*Tilia* spp.) reaching forwards.

Left: The striking panelling, exposed beams and mullion windows of the parlour do not need elaborate furniture.

Below left: The patina of the mahogany chairs, oak panelling and worn carpet come from age and cannot be reproduced.

Below right: Kipling's writing equipment still lies on the chestnut desk in the study, which has been preserved as it was in the writer's time, complete with his collection of books.

Furniture that is about the same period as the house never dates. Although there is little in the other rooms in the house to serve as reminders of Kipling's childhood in India, the crewelwork material of the curtains could well have come from there. Such fabrics are still exported and are ideal for country houses. Here, they make an excellent complement for both the furniture and the embroidered bed hangings.

be out of place now, at the end of the twentieth century or even at the end of the twenty-first century. It is a timeless, comfortable, country house, which, apart from the benefits of electricity, central heating and modern sanitation, is much as it always was and could always be. Fashion is by its very nature a transient thing and many a ruined house litters its erratic path. Good taste, by contrast, knows when to leave well alone.

The inner hall retains all the architectural detail of the house's earliest years – the panelling, the beams and the staircase. A faded verdure tapestry is hung from the first floor. The tapestry and a bowl of fresh flowers against the patina of a highly polished cupboard are all the decoration that is needed. The parlour has its floorboards and oak panelling still. A couple of oak barley twist carvers sit in front of the stone-mullioned windows, and a sagging old Knole settee stands in front of the fire. In the corner is a Georgian wing chair beside a Tiffany lamp, their curves complementing one another. There is nothing about this room that requires alteration. It would not look any better for wallpaper above the panelling, for example. The only possible improvements might be new curtains to hang within the window and cushioning for the window seat. They need not be new fabric, however; recycled tapestry or crewel work would be admirable. If the Knole settee were not to your taste, you might consider replacing it with something plain and plump. But these are additional niceties – the room does not actually require them.

The dining room also works extremely well as it is. Notice how the chinoiserie colours of the paper behind the table blend with the those of the carpet and the panel above the fireplace, and see how the blue ground of the needlepoint to the dining chairs and their stylized flowers echo those of the paper. Certainly, the carpet is faded and worn, the paper is coming away a little, but a glossy, new perfection would not be appropriate here and would sit oddly with the house. It would, if one were honest, be tempting to return the fireplace to its former glory

and to remove those copper jugs. The Chippendale chairs, although, like the paper and carpet, later than the house itself, speak of generations passing through the same house.

The library is simply the library: it looks exactly as it should do with its rows of shelves, the old table and rugs, and the library chair. If Kipling were alive now, it would probably contain a computer or word processor – he was rather keen on the latest inventions – but nothing else need change.

Upstairs are the crewelwork curtains that might have hung downstairs, together with a barley twist four-poster and day-bed, embroidered hangings and bedspread. The simplicity of the embroidery, the lack of pretension to the straight lines of the material, although of a later date, are all in keeping with the period of the house and the bed-head. Quantities of ruched silk would look very out of place here.

Local vernacular in tile hanging provides the cladding for two original oast-house towers, now converted to domestic use.

Right: A grouping of pink *Diascia* with grey *Lamium* leaves and blue *Echinops* heads provide a colourful incident within the garden.

Outside, the oast-houses, which were originally used for drying hops, have become decorative. One has a dovecote on top, the other has had its height reduced. The clay tile hanging right to the ground is an interesting piece of local vernacular architecture, which is repeated in the entrance to what has now become the National Trust shop.

Batemans is an interesting combination of country buildings and country garden bones on the small scale, for it is very much a composition based on line and mass, the very basis of good design. Plants have been used structurally to extend the lines of the house, putting out feelers into the surrounding land. The garden has been kept much as it was in Kipling's time, with mixed borders of shrubs and herbaceous in yellows and whites, to pinks and blues. These are the soft colours of English country gardens. If they were (or could be) used in hotter climates, under harsher lights, they would lose their lustral qualities and fade into insignificance. Bright light requires bight flowers and vice versa. There has also to be a gentle fading

away into the surrounding land, rather than a strong, dramatic contrast with it.

A line of pleached limes continues the three-dimensional approach at Batemans. Changes of level, a sort of mini ha-ha, strengthen the building line and work with the pleached limes. The borders are all of an English floriferousness in summer, but there is also a sparseness about it that is very attractive. It is, in fact, what a good garden should be all about in winter, for in summer a design's strength is all but concealed by the broad masses of planting that overlay the structure. It is important, too, that the masses of more flowery material – whether shrub, herb or perennial – are used in large enough quantities to be in scale with the framework of the scheme, its setting and the house it surrounds.

Kipling's own garden was less stately, although a miniature of those he vaunted. In his own words:

Our England is a garden that is full of stately views
Of borders, beds and shrubberies and lawns and avenues.
Nevertheless they required an immense amount of work:
Our England is a garden, and such gardens are not made
By singing 'Oh, how beautiful and sitting in the shade'.

Batemans is a wonderful example of the good ground rules that are needed for country garden planning, and those rules may be re-interpreted in many different styles and locations.

Above: A wheelbarrow full of geraniums with golden privet behind do not instantly appeal as a grouping, but in reality, against a red tile-hung wall, they form an eye-catching structural association of plants.

Left: Yew hedges provide green alternatives to stone walls, so that this vital structural element of the garden becomes a continuation of the building proportions it adjoins.

COTTAGE STYLE

Our vision of the archetypal cottage has been coloured by the archetypal scene of roses round the door – roses planted for the most part in the late nineteenth century. What were once the humble dwelling of agricultural labourers have come to evoke a picture of whitewashed purity, complete with leaded lights, a thatched roof and a ribbon of blue smoke from the chimney. Inside are beams and bread ovens, chintz curtains fluttering at the windows, patchwork quilts and overstuffed sofas. There is a garden path edged with lavender, a square of closely mown lawn and borders of 'old favourites' – spires of larkspur, clumps of pinks and a haze of love-in-the-mist. We imagine that there will be an apple tree and perhaps a row of lettuces, but the romantic imagination often fails to come up with the more prosaic and prickly currant bushes and outdoor privy.

The reality, then and now, can be different. The crofts of Ireland and the Highlands of Scotland were mostly stone-built, and many had only one or two rooms and a small window. The smoke from a peat fire would rise, in the humblest and earliest cottages, through a hole in the roof, which was thatched with turf or heather. Longer crofts were shared with the livestock, providing warmth for both family and animals in the winter. There was little furniture, and clothes were hung on a few nails in the wall. Lilian Beckwith describes her Hebridean croft cottage in 1961 as having a kitchen leading off one side of the entrance porch and 'the room' off the other:

> In Bruach this second room was never known as anything but 'the room', presumably because no one was really sure of its intended purpose. ... In many of the single-storeyed croft houses these two rooms, with a recessed bed in the kitchen, comprised the whole of the living accommodation. Yet in such limited space large families were reared and a galaxy of scholars produced. It was no unusual sight to see a university student at his books by the light of a

candle in a corner of the small kitchen, while all around him the neighbours jostled and gossiped, argued and sang.

Vernacular architecture is dependent on the needs of the inhabitants and the materials available to them. The timber frame, lath and plaster construction and straw thatch of a Buckinghamshire cottage, will be replaced by granite under a slate roof in Wales. The fertility of the land, its climate, its irrigation and its exposure will dictate the potential of its garden. You can no more expect gillyflowers and cherry blossom in the Hebrides than bougainvillaea in Norfolk. There may be other problems for the gardener, too. Alice Thomas Ellis's idyll of *A Welsh Childhood* in the 1950s was lived in:

> a cottage on the top road between the Iron Age axe factory of Graiglwyd and the granite quarry. ... We had a small front garden with a little wooden gate and a slate path. There was a lilac tree on the left with banks of snow-in-summer growing underneath it. On the right was a fuchsia hedge and my mother tried to grow dahlias but the sheep used to jump down the wall from the mountain and eat them.

The cottage idylls painted by Helen Allingham and Myles Birket Foster towards the end of the last century were not built of dark granite under slate roofs. Theirs were the cottages of Suffolk and Oxfordshire, whitewashed and thatched or Cotswold stone and stone slate, built to house the agricultural labourers who worked for the manor house.

When J. Arthur Gibbs described *A Cotswold Village* in 1898, he marvelled at the architectural perfection,

Above right: The picket fence with rambler roses and honeysuckle (*Lonicera* spp.) around the door are all part of a British cottage-garden style. This is a slate-roofed nineteenth-century cottage.

Below right: Plain white walls and dragged paintwork are simple and appropriate decorations for a cottage interior.

Making beer was a common country practice, and many a previous malthouse has been converted into a fine cottage dwelling. The barrel on the right was not, of course, originally for decoration.

the simplicity and grace, with not a gable or chimney that would not be worthy of a place in the Royal Academy. He admired the great Cotswold tithe barns, which he mistook at first sight for churches and which were often built with even more attention to architectural detail – Gothic windows, massive buttresses and elaborate pinnacles – in deference to their importance for the life and lives of the estate. They were all 'strong and lasting' – and for the most part constructed between 1600 and 1700.

Mindful of the value of an agricultural wage, Gibbs marvelled at the efforts of the cottagers, remarking on the spotless cleanliness of their houses, their homely comforts, the neatness and good taste in the way the children were dressed for church on Sunday, and the pride the cottagers took in their gardens. They were indeed the very stuff of romance:

What a charm there is in an old-fashioned English garden! The great tall hollyhocks and phlox, the bright orange marigolds and large purple poppies. The beds and borders crammed with cloves and many-coloured asters, the sweet blue of the cornflower, and the little lobelias.

Yet not 80 kilometres (50 miles) away and within the same generation, Flora Thompson recalled a different picture in *Lark Rise to Candleford*:

A few of the houses had thatched roofs, whitewashed outer walls and diamond-paned windows, but the majority were just stone or brick boxes with

blue-slated roofs. ... In nearly all the cottages there was but one room downstairs, and many of these were poor and bare, with only a table and a few chairs and stools for furniture and a superannuated potato-sack thrown down by way of hearthrug.

Nevertheless, every house had a good vegetable garden, and there were allotments for all. Her grandfather would come every morning bringing 'a little basket of early raspberries or green peas, already shelled, or a tight little bunch of sweet williams and moss rosebuds, or a baby rabbit'.

If there is one principle that obtains in the decoration of cottages it is respect for their architectural integrity and origins. The same rule applies to the cultivation of the cottage garden. As its original purpose was subsistence, fruit and vegetables are a natural part of it. Traditionally it would have had beaten earth or ash paths leading from the door to a number of regular plots, which enabled a simple, annual rotation of crops. Herbs were as much a constituent of the cottage garden as vegetables, partly

A modern cottage vegetable garden that contains curly kale and spring onions, with blue pickling cabbage and maize. The right-hand screen is covered with runner beans. There is also a forcing jar for rhubarb and a beehive at the end of the plot.

At the end of the twentieth century the cottage and its garden have become a second or holiday home.
They are pastoral retreats from the stresses of urban living.

because of their use as medical remedies and partly because they were used as a natural means of deterring insects and plant diseases. Companion plantings of, say, parsley to ward off carrot fly or summer savory to keep beans free of aphids is both pretty and useful. This working layout is not peculiar to Britain. It is found, with obvious cultural and climatic differences, in more or less every country.

While early cottage gardening in Britain was to do with planting, in America it was to do with clearing. The early American vegetable garden, for example, was often separate from the cottage since the house itself was shaded by trees in the hot summers. Cottage gardening in the Mediterranean countries cannot permit the delicate pastels and lush foliage that need regular rainfall. But plumbago scrambling in cerulean blue over a whitewashed wall will make as good as any alternative to the velvet-petalled clematis.

Today, the term cottage garden allows for a certain 'controlled' disorganization: a collection of bright flowers, vegetables and herbs growing together without any overall planting design. Vogues and fashion alter the look from time to time, with box edging sometimes introduced as a hark-back to the seventeenth century, or with lavender masses, an enthusiasm from Provence, or white roses as part of a trend to the 'single colour' garden.

When the vogue for exotic planting, garish colour and the bedding out of half-hardy plants threatened to swamp the villas and grander gardens of nineteenth-century Britain, turning Repton's 'picturesque' into Loudon's 'gardenesque', William Robinson and later Gertrude Jekyll resorted to the cottage garden as antidote. Only in cottage gardens, observed Robinson in *The English Flower Garden*, could flowers be seen growing in a pleasing and natural way. 'Cottage gardens have a simple and tender charm that one may look for in vain in gardens of greater pretension,' wrote Jekyll. 'And the old garden flowers seem to know that there they are seen at their best.'

THATCHED COTTAGE

A little gravel path winds between clumps of lavender, bushes of rosemary and spires of sunny verbascum up to the doors of the sitting room in the white cottage under the low, thatched roof. As you walk between the old-fashioned herbs, your hands and clothes brush against their leaves, taking on their sweet, dry scents, while all about you the air is filled with the intoxicating fragrance of roses.

There are some gardens that are, in effect, extensions of their houses: they are garden rooms. The outside is part of the inside. This is the other way about. The garden is so perfect an example of the romantic cottage style that it will take you to the house as if it were yet another border or an arbour or a summerhouse.

Inside, reminders of the garden are all about you, most obviously in the jugs and jars of fresh flowers – daisies and ladies' mantle on the kitchen table, roses by the bedside and a jar of cow parsley, or, to give it its much prettier common name, Queen Anne's lace, picked straight from the hedgerow to stand beside a hanging row of old rolling pins.

This is not a house for elaborate, fussy or formal flower arrangements. There are no exotic orchids strained by years of selective breeding, there are no dyed carnations and no chrysanthemums, wired to hang at precise angles. Just as the garden flowers are without pretension, so are those in the house.

The theme is followed in the house itself. The colours are light and natural, the furniture pleasing and of sturdy simplicity. Cream is used in the kitchen for the walls. The wainscoting has been left *in situ* and painted white, like the open shelves. It lifts the room and adds a lightness that it would not otherwise have. Crisp white linen on the circular pedestal table and strong Windsor chairs combine to keep a traditional feel. The floorboards

Above: A gravelled surface runs up to the doors of the sitting room of this cottage allowing an entirely appropriate loose planting of herbs and perennials.

Right: There is little about the eating end of the kitchen that would have been different a century ago. It is made light by the use of pale colours, simple by the use of gathered cotton, fresh by flowers and traditional by the Windsor chairs.

Left: Common wildflowers, including violet, columbine and Queen Anne's lace (cow parsley), bring the land in which the cottage is set into the house itself.

Right: A backless, drop-end sofa, which can double as a day- or night-bed frames the window which, in turn, provides a frame for the sofa.

Below right: The latched, planked door and deeply recessed window are reminders that this is a cottage, so that the introduction of contemporary touches, like the smart but simple stripes of the bed linen, can be used to give the room a lively, up-to-date look that is not out of place.

have been simply sanded and varnished, which is a practical and attractive treatment.

The sitting room is washed in cream, and the lath and plaster ceiling between the exposed oak beams is white. One wall is exposed stone, less exposed now that it, too, has been washed and covered with a collection of old prints. How much darker, how much more raw and cold it would have looked without its cream wash. A Georgian armchair, upholstered in ivory damask, and a plump, dark floral sofa make this a comfortable

room. Warmth is also given by the colour of the chintz curtains – rosy roses that are reflections of the garden when the real things are in bloom, reminders of summer when they are not.

Of course, the French doors to the sitting room were not there 300 years ago when the house was built. Glass was expensive then and French doors were only for grander houses. Most of the windows in the cottage would have been smaller then, too, not only because of the expense but also because the house needed to be kept cool in the summer

and warm in the winter. But we do not easily tolerate darkness nowadays, and central heating warms our winters – and it must be admitted that the added light is attractive and that the additional views of the garden do give another dimension to a room.

Most of this cottage's rooms are traditional in mood. The exception is the guest bedroom, which has been treated to a snappier, more contemporary look that is not at odds in any way with the old house but enlivens it in an amusing, witty way by just a few discreet touches. The exposed beams and the old door with its heavy latch have been retained. The door is painted white. The casement is small, but instead of curtains a small simple white blind has been used, a modern touch that reveals, just as curtains would have disguised, the depth of the recess and hence the age of the old walls. A pine and canvas director's chair, and striking stripy bed linen are modern furnishings. Together with the jaunty panama hanging on the back of the door, they add a light, cheerful air to the room without disturbing its essential structural qualities.

Just as cottages in general are often turned into a clutter of bric-à-brac, so their gardens have become victims of excessive decoration, the upward thrust of snobbery dragging urns and balustrades into what  was originally a working layout for the purpose of subsistence. What is cheering about this cottage garden is that it demonstrates a clarity of decorative intention while remaining faithful to its traditions.

The long walk away from the French windows takes you deeper into the garden, to a rectangle of lawn surrounded on three sides by borders. Although they are planted for the most part on the age-old principle of tallest at the back, shortest at the front, the odd exception to the rule is diverting. *Alchemilla mollis* (lady's mantle) makes a soft

Above: The garden can be enjoyed from a brick-paved seating area at the end of the lawn. The flowering plant is a tree peony, with a gold-leafed euonymus nearby.

Right: A healthy vegetable garden is part of the cottage scene. Its foliage colours and shapes are colourful and attractive. The fluffy foliage is asparagus.

Opposite: The sophistication of this planting, although based on cottage-garden principles, is now almost country house in scale. Note the vertical emphasis of lupin and delphinium, which provide a regular rhythm through the lower masses of planting.

edging, which is particularly useful in a cottage garden where clipped dwarf box would have a more rigid formality. Here the soft green leaves and lime green, frothy inflorescence spill on to the grass, broken by the salmon pink heads of aquilegia, carried on high, slender stems. Its very fragility is reason alone to plant this at the front of the border, but it seeds itself so profusely that you may find it everywhere. The lime flowers of lady's mantle are echoed, deeper in the border, by the lime buttons of the euphorbia, which, together with the touches of gold foliage, make a good contrast with the mauve-blue delphiniums and deep red lupins.

At the bottom of the garden, on the left of the lawn, is a sunny sitting place, a little rectangular terrace made of old red brick surrounded by stone troughs, and at its corner is a magnificent tree peony. At the opposite end is a small pool, fed from the stream that runs along the bottom of the fields behind the garden. Here is a small bog garden, for plants such as marsh marigold,

candelabra primulas, ferns and the delicate green and white heads of *Astrantia major*. A few steps further, and you are led to the vegetable garden, two rectangular plots neatly planted with wigwams for runner beans, rows of onions and fattening pods of broad beans. The second plot, more potager than vegetable alone, is filled with a mix of fruit and flowers and vegetables – the puce and purple of brassicas, the golds and orange of poppies and marigolds – and is a productive move back towards the side of the cottage, in keeping with the herbs and flowers nearer the house.

TUSCAN CONVERSION

The rough track – you would scarcely call it a road – lurches and twists, pothole after pothole, through the glorious undulations of Tuscan hillsides, terraced with vines, shady with olives, magnificent with cypress. The light that envelops the surrounding hills is lustrous and blue, and the air is sweet and clear as a farmer hoes between his rows of vines. It is all so evocative – just as we imagine a pastoral paradise. Poverty in a land of great natural beauty can appear so charming.

This old farm cottage, stone-built under a clay-tiled roof, has had a face-lift, borrowing ideas from grander gardens on the one hand and playing peasant on the other. It sits on a gentle hill – its view of the olive terraces and the grander stone house opposite is unchanged for a thousand years, perhaps longer. We know of Roman gardens in Tuscany and the pleasure they too found in their restorative qualities.

The face-lift inside the cottage has for the most part been prophylactic – relaying floors, shoring up timbers – and the improvements were mostly

Above: A typical Tuscan landscape, which has probably been cultivated for two thousand years or so. The hillsides are terraced for the cultivation of both vines and olives.

Right: This room may once have been used to house farm animals in winter or to store grain. Now, large windows and the brick floor and original roof give the room an inside-outside feel, while the painted decorations on the doors echo its current use.

Right and far right: Art, in the form of pictures – either hung on the walls or as decoration on the doors – or in the form of ceramics – pots or sculptures – are the only decoration this house needs. They emphasize and enhance its clean lines.

confined to wiring and plumbing. The old beams have been left as they are, and the old, uneven, rough plastered walls have been re-whitewashed. The architectural integrity of the house has not been interfered with in any way. The doors are mostly double doors. Where they were simple latched timber planks they have been left as such; where they were panelled, they have been left panelled. Some of the walls and doors have been painted with animals and birds and flowers and trees. There is the odd, witty reminder of a Roman past in this – and it is very attractive. At the same time it manages to evoke an ephemeral feel, for the decoration will fade with the passage of time, but the very fabric and the essential structure of the house has been preserved as it was and will survive longer. It has something of the same quality of the murals of trees and birds and flowers preserved on Roman walls at Pompeii and Herculaneum, and we feel something of the same thrill when we see contemporary re-creations.

There is plenty of wall painting in the bedrooms – birds and fountains, trees and Doric columns. Representations of the countryside on the walls are accompanied by the realities of what this countryside brings – mosquitoes. The nets suspended from the ceiling are there for good reason. Coloured throws and cushions, and woven and embroidered hangings from a brass pole give the room its warmth. Together with an old chest, a not-so-old chest of drawers and some painted furniture preserve the simple, peasant feel.

In the kitchen the cooking is still done in the old chimney breast, although not on a fire, and painted tiles, suitably timeless, decorate the rear wall where the opening would have been. An old dresser stands at one side, a dresser of some sort probably always has. It is all quite practical and unpretentious.

This cottage has been used to reflect a number of interests in the lives of its owners. Despite its simplicity and the clear desire not to stray too far from the vernacular nature of its origins, it adapts happily to the books, painting and sculpture – the witty recollections of classical antiquity – with a practicality and balance of handling. Lose that balance – by overdoing one or other aspect – and it would all become a little far-fetched. The study, for

The study contains reminders of antiquity, with detailed plasterwork and a nymph.

Left: The building's original deep, wide casement windows make the bedroom seem light and spacious, bringing the outside in. The walls have been decorated with pretty murals – wallpaper would have been wholly inappropriate.

Above: Corner bowls have been typical here for thousands of years. This one comes with modern plumbing.

Right: Positioning the bath in the centre of the room is one way of showing that this room was not originally intended as a bathroom. Again, the decoration takes the form of paintings hung on the walls, and there has been no attempt to introduce ceramic tiles or any of the other trappings of the 'designer' bathroom.

A vine-covered softwood pergola provides summer shade. In winter, when the leaves have dropped, the pergola provides a measure of wind shelter, but now allows the sunlight through.

example, is mostly about books. Hints of antiquity that we saw in the murals are here made plastic: a Doric column scratched in the plaster work, and one of the Three Graces perching on top of the bookcase. It is amusing and charming and does not seriously dent the original nature of the house. Overdo the classic theme, however, and you have over-kill. There is just enough here to bring a smile.

The garden surrounding this cottage has also retained its genuine quality, although quite clearly its status has improved.

The vine features heavily, for in its decorative green shade summer life is lived outside, as cool hilltop breezes brush the setting. Supporting the

vines is a simple structure of softwood poles – a type the Romans might have made – and it provides an interesting transition from the method of stringing the vines employed on the surrounding hillsides, helping to meld the cottage into its setting. The stone table is set for a lazy lunch, and there are pots massed around it, filled with scented-leaf geraniums as well as the more floriferous types. But notice that the pots are hardly visible under the weight of foliage. Everything is understated. We tend to use pots as decorative ornaments – the countryman uses them to contain.

The entrance to the cottage runs seductively under olives and down a grassy path lined with

box balls in pots. This is touch of sophistication in the 'gardened' part of the garden, and you can see immediately that it will need watering.

Cottage style, wherever it is found in the world, was honed by practicality and by a lack of both money and pretension. It has an earthy rightness about it, which we can appreciate from the sophistication of our urbanized lives but find difficult to achieve – for we have been spoiled for choice. This is a tranquil example, where indulgence has been curbed, and the result embodies all the seductive qualities of a Tuscan holiday home. For we can only visit another lifestyle – it would be impossible to live the dream.

Above: A fantasy lunch setting, which has left its cottage origins long since. The stone table and metal chairs do, however, have a good, earthy stability.

Left: Terracotta is native to this part of the world, and most wonderful pots are available. This mixed planting includes the white-flower angel's trumpet (*Datura* spp.), which is very poisonous. A peach tree grows against the wall behind this setting.

STONE COTTAGE

This Oxfordshire cottage of brick and limestone under a Stonesfield slate roof feels larger than the archetypal cottage, and the difference is apparent in the large, light windows and the lack of a series of small dark rooms. Instead, there are two large main rooms on the ground floor – a kitchen-cum-dining room and a sitting room. What is interesting about it is that it uses all the trappings normally associated with small cottages in such a way as to make them appear more interesting than when they are confined in a small space. At the same time, the sense of space allows for the use of pieces normally associated with much grander houses. The same feeling is reflected in the garden: there is a sense of space, the use of traditional cottage garden plants and the incorporation of some features that would be at home in grander or more exotic gardens.

As soon as you enter this cottage you become immediately aware of these themes, and of others, for there are clues to the interests of the owners everywhere we look. For a start, there are the big

Above: The garden to this cottage contains the correct muddle of climbers, herbs and perennials. You step out into a wonderful jungle, which asks to be explored.

Right: A large country cottage will support an eclectic mix of furnishings, especially when they are brought together and dominated by a unifying architectural feature, such as these red-painted ceiling joists.

Left: In this cottage the kitchen also serves as the dining room and study. A great deal of work is done around the edges of the room, which are unified by putting the focus on the large, circular table in the centre.

earthenware jars under the hall table that are flour bins. Whether they contain flour is irrelevant – they have already created the expectation of some good home-made, stone-ground bread. There are old wooden carvings, there are paintings, there is a headless, armless bust and a beaten metal Indian pot – a diverse range of interests and strong artistic sense are obvious. Then again, everything points to a love of the country and time spent outside, for why else should there be a collection of walking-sticks and of straw hats for working in the garden?

As for the borrowed finery of grander houses, the old rope-framed overmantel mirror seems perfectly at home in humbler quarters. Its condition is not exactly pristine, which is just as well. A perfect example of shining gilded gesso would have looked and felt uncomfortable. The way the walls are painted embodies this mix of grand and humble. The colour is a cross between

'Germolene' pink and Umbrian orange, both colours favoured in historic houses, but it has been roughly brushed, in deference to the simplicity of its setting and in keeping with the old stone-flagged floor. And the colour warms up the cold stone beautifully.

The sitting room is a lovely jumble of colour and period styles. Bright ethnic rugs, throws over modern sofas, a collection of antique clocks, a flap-top bureau and an old grand piano are brought together under the red-painted beams picked out against a white ceiling. It is this last touch that unites the room. Because it is such a bright red, the eye is immediately drawn to it, so as you enter you know that this is going to be no ordinary sitting room. It prepares you for an interest in all the other details, the furniture and the furnishings, what is used as ornament and what takes place here. Reading, writing, chess and music embody

Light streams through the large dormer window onto the stairwell and landing. The banister rail and balusters are simple and unadorned, allowing attention to focus on the paintings and prints with which the walls are covered.

the character of the house. It is not dressed for an occasion by an anonymous designer; it is the real expression of the interests of interesting people.

The kitchen/dining room bears the same stamp. As you come in through the wide latched door there is a collection of well-used rakes, gardening gloves, baskets and trugs, and more gardening hats, all kept dry and to hand beside the warmth of the old continental stove. This is not clutter for effect, and hence meaningless; it is clutter to a real purpose.

The collection of chairs set around the sturdy circular pedestal dining table is further proof of the partnership between grand and simple – rosewood, mahogany and bentwood. The same eclecticism is seen on the shelves, where fine china mixes with contemporary pottery, silver with mugs. And there are paintings and books and statuettes and jam pans – no one could be bored or boring here.

On the whole, most cluttered cottages repel scrutiny. Lots of small pieces of furniture, too many china ornaments and not enough books or paintings make a cottage appear twee. Overloaded with that sort of thing the mind becomes clogged. In this cottage, however, the mind is opened. By mixing grand with practical and by using a few big pieces – overmantels, table, piano – the smaller objects are thrown into relief. Everything then compels scrutiny.

This house, the Clock House, is, in fact, part of the outbuildings of a former, much larger house, which was burnt down. You can still see the foundations and the layout of the ground-floor rooms in the turf. The cottage itself was part stable, part bothy (where the unmarried stable lads and garden boys used to live).

The land on which the big house used to sit is divided from the Clock House by a small lane. On

Above: The old wooden boards used for the deep sill and part of the work surface make a pleasingly continuous transition between the cottage exterior, the window and the interior.

Left: A little greenhouse is tucked into the corner of the garden for bringing on seeds, with a cold frame beside it. The huge central plant with green flowers is *Euphorbia wulfenii*; beyond it is a white-flowering *Crambe cordifolia*.

Over the garden wall there is a beautiful dovecote, while in the garden itself, biennial poppies (*Papaver* spp.) seed themselves all over the place, popping up through cracks in the paving and among longer living perennials.

this side the Clock House faces into a paved yard. The real garden is at the back, overlooked by the kitchen and sitting room. It is not large, but it evokes all the senses engendered by the description – a walled garden.

Its late, much missed owner, the photographer Michael Whickham, and his wife, Denni, have pottered in this garden for many a year, and like a good wine, it is now full and rich with favourite plants. Old-fashioned roses climb up between door and window. Between the cracks in the stone paving clumps of white feverfew, mounds of sweet, bright, pink *Geranium endressii*, and the soft, downy grey leaves of *Stachys lanata* (lamb's tongue) have been allowed to dispose themselves where they will. Almost a bush by now, euphorbia, with its blue-green tiers of leaves and lime green bracts, has been established for years. Further on the

garden is high with carmine poppies and royal purple clematis, set off by white and pink roses and the rich deep blue of cornflowers. One of the loveliest trees in the garden, with its long blue-grey green leaf, is *Hippophae rhamnoides* (sea buckthorn) – 'the nearest you can get in this country', Michael once said, 'to an olive'.

The permanent table and chairs outside are testimony to many wonderful meals eaten outside. So, too, are the groupings of herbs, beneath the flower masses, grown all mixed up with shrub roses and perennials. Beyond the walled enclosure, the Whickhams gardened over the lane as well, growing vegetables and more flowers between the foundations of the big house. This was their way with late twentieth-century *laisser-faire* gardening, but it is a way that is entirely appropriate in a much older setting.

Annual wild poppies self-seed at the side of a lime walk (*Tilia* spp.). This piece of garden is over a lane from the cottage and its walled enclosure.

The far garden contains vegetables, but there are yet more oriental poppies, which are perennial. The white flowers are of *Crambe*, which has rather coarse, large leaves.

Flowers and foliage couch the cottage, the old stone wall encloses it, and, beyond, a tall circular dovecote overlooks it. You see the butterflies, you hear the bees and the great glorious flowerheads force their welcome attentions on you. It is all of a piece with its setting, its harmonies flowing from the inside out, from the outside in. The same strong sense of style that allowed the beautiful, the interesting and the useful to find their place inside the house has been used outside to create the groupings that make for cottage garden perfection. What might seem random has been carefully thought through, and more importantly, allowed to flourish. For a good eye not only conceives a relationship with plants, but controls it in maturity, too. We are so attuned to a constant chiding to maintain a garden, and sold the machinery, feeds and sprays with which to do it, that to know when to leave well alone has become an art in itself. It is lovely to experience a garden that has not been chivvied into suburban conformity.

MAJORCAN FINCA

Getting on for a thousand years old, this *finca* was a traditional Majorcan dwelling for farm labourers. The rooms under the roof upstairs would have been used to store grain, while the two principal rooms for human habitation were the kitchen with its vast fireplace and the hall.

Some fifteen years ago it was bought by Miguel Servera, director of the Miro Foundation in Palma. He has kept faith with the building's simplicity. Most of the walls are roughly plastered and white-washed, the floors are unobtrusively tiled in earth colours and the mats are sisal, and the old cupboard niches have been left unaltered. In return, the house has offered a wonderful foil for a collection of old and contemporary paintings.

The external elevation is pure vernacular and an essay in the harmony of local materials. The walls and steps are rough limestone, the door surrounds are plain dressed limestone, and even the down pipe seems to be stone. The big, arched double front door of old timber planks and nails is a later addition, but it, too, seems comfortable in its

surroundings. The size of the arch and the cobble floor infill suggest an earlier use as stable or byre. All the windows, both the original small windows and the later, bigger ones, have a traditional white surround, which not only defines their spaces and the spaces in between but also has the effect of making them appear larger.

Inside, the sitting room is plainly furnished and decorated. Whitewashed walls, exposed beams and a shelved alcove reflect the depth of the thick stone walls and call attention to the architectural elements of the room, to the mural by Guinovard, and his *trompe l'œil* plates on the shelves behind the pottery and glass. The mural and plates

Above: Traditional builders had to use the local stone – nothing else was available – and the unity that this restriction imposed on their building is very obvious in the courtyard of this Majorcan *finca*.

Right: The new stone arch, with its clean, dramatic curve, has replaced the dividing wall, thereby more than doubling the available space and allowing the two floors to flow into each other, despite the change in level.

account for the majority of the colour in the room, but it is sparingly used. The simplicity of the few pieces of furniture – a large low pine table, a local pine settee flanked by a very old timber box on one side and a chest on the other – is deliberate. More opulent or more decorative pieces would have detracted from the art and the structure and would have sat uneasily with the origins of the building.

The dining room follows much the same principles. By using plain, railed, rush-seated chairs about a sturdy dining table on turned legs under a metal chandelier, Servera is conforming to local, unostentatious tradition. Even the tablecloth is local. Under the table is an old footwarmer. Beside the glazed door is a small marble basin and tap. The blue glass goblets and pottery plates and dishes are also all local.

In the old kitchen the stone architrave has been left unpainted, making a frame between this and the adjoining room. Old blue painted tiles, ancient utensils and contemporary wooden spoons in the

same tradition furnish the alcove, while the simple painted dishes on the shelf above complete the decoration. More pots and dishes and an antique Majorcan amphora sit on shelves and niches. Countless small salamis hang from the white-washed beams. In the large, basket-wrapped jars

Opposite above: The adroit placing of decorative elements, pictures and furniture emphasizes the horizontal lines imposed by the beams and by the shelves in the alcove.

Opposite below left: The use of traditional, local furniture keeps the *finca* firmly rooted in its time and place.

Opposite below right: The original stone architrave around the interior kitchen door has been left unpainted, and the decoration is provided by local pottery and painted tiles.

Right: Partitioning is a good solution when space is needed for other purposes. Again, the use of local furniture and materials, including Majorcan lace, anchor the *finca* in the island's traditions.

on the floor are preserved quantities of different olives, much as they always have been.

It is only by looking at kitchens like this that one appreciates the practicality, the simplicity and basic good taste bestowed by the past. The idea of disguising the old shelves and alcoves, of fixing ubiquitous units and laminated 'work surfaces' to the walls is unthinkable. It would dishonour the work of old artisans for whom the best is best left alone.

The bedrooms are calm and peaceful. Inlaid and carved Majorcan bedsteads dressed in white with lace-trimmed bedspreads of local manufacture are the main ornaments of the room. They pay tribute to the artistry of the island and to the domestic crafts of which its people are rightly proud.

The floor, which was once the granary, has been turned into one large room, bare except for the mural depicting the history of the *finca* by Felix de Cardenas, and a small dresser built by local craftsmen, which has been painted without artifice to reflect the blue, green and grey of its homeland.

The cobbled yard is kept plain, overhung by an

Geraniums are stacked beside a door under a great bougainvillea. Note how even the downspout to the right is made of carved stone.

old olive tree. Only the corner of the building allows for decoration: a purple bougainvillea reaches for the roof, its depth of colour complementing the mellowed stone of the walls while the old stone water toughs are brimming with geraniums.

In the garden behind the house the same respect has been paid to the past. The vital importance of water and the luxury of one's own well meant that the well-head often became the central feature of the courtyard. In this case, the well-head is the focal point of the pergola, made welcoming by the dappled shade of the vine. The columns and paving are of the same limestone used throughout, with whitewashed timber horizontals supporting the vine. In summer, when it is in leaf the vine

gives shade; in winter, when the leaves have dropped, the sunlight gets through to warm this little garden.

Drystone walls and low-key terracotta pots continue the theme of local simplicity but the over-riding mood is of light and shade. The lack of distraction of flowers or over-ornamented containers, the concentration on green foliage and stonework and the play of light make for peace and tranquillity in this outdoor room.

This is a house of humble origins, built with self-respect and incorporating the values of plain, decent, solid labour. In its transition to contemporary life it has saluted those origins and permitted a happy marriage between the past and contemporary art and craft.

Above: The well was the hub of a country dwelling, for without water neither man nor his cattle survived. This well head is beautifully shaded by a pergola, which is supported by vertical stone piers.

Left: The dream setting, which would originally have looked out over the peasant's fields. From here, he could keep an eye on the land below and, in the evening, take wine.

FIFTEENTH-CENTURY COTTAGE

Black and White Cottage is 500 years old. It stands at the end of a winding lane in a 4-hectare (10-acre) garden, straddling a rushing brook and surrounded by venerable oaks and reddening Scots pines. Landscape designer Anthony Paul turned the land into a water garden, with four large pools through which the brook flows under timber decking for walkways, causeways and bridges. There are green glades under the massive trees for contemplation, and the lush planting of the giant foliage of gunnera and petasites for the thrill of the unfamiliar. Twelve years ago his partner Hannah Peschar decided to use it as an outdoor gallery for three-dimensional art, and it is now one of the leading galleries for contemporary sculpture and ceramics. Taken together, the cottage, the sculpture garden and their setting all pay homage to nature and art.

Above: A deck hangs out over the water, and its strong horizontal line is contrasted with the verticality of a weeping willow and with the huge leaves of a *Gunnera manicata*.

Left: The plain woodblock floor and exposed bricks complement the oak beams.

You approach the north face of the cottage between two reaches of water. The mossy brick path is simply planted on either side and rests between great mounds of evergreen. The front door is flanked by loose, unclipped box trees with their sprays of tiny dark green leaves, and from autumn through to spring a large *Viburnum* x *burkwoodii* brings the sweet scent of its pale pink florets into the house as you enter.

The cottage is tiny but it has a spacious feel. 'It is a very small space', says Hannah. 'But I like to see the lines of its structure. I want to emphasize the architecture, to have it predominate rather than obscuring it with a mass of fabric and drapes and furniture. I wanted to create spaces, an atmosphere where there are no obstacles.'

They had everything to do in the house – rewiring, central heating, and new kitchen and bathroom. 'It was in a dreadful state but the basic structure was sound.' Just how sound it was they came to realize in the terrible gales of 1987, when they lost 25 trees in the garden but scarcely a roof tile.

One end of the sitting room provides a clean, uncluttered space for the brilliant flames of their modern paintings. At the other end burn the logs in a fireplace that has seen fires since the sixteenth century. Its original lining is still there, dented and hollowed by centuries of knife sharpening against its surface. Even the old hanging irons for cooking pots and smoking hams remain, alongside the bread oven. A parchment coloured Berber carpet throughout the room extends the space, as does the pale almond wash to the walls. The use of single, pale colours throws into relief the details of the beams, which are decoration enough. The eighteenth-century oak pedestal table is Dutch. It faces the curly-armed chair on the other side, which was bought from Devon furniture-maker Paul Anderson, whose work Hannah also exhibits in the sculpture garden.

The kitchen has a cooking end and a dining end. A stud partition once divided the two. When it was removed a stout oak supporting post was revealed. It had to be left, of course, but it makes a fitting minimal boundary between the two areas. Both the oak trestle table and the cupboard units were made from the couple's own trees. 'But ecologically correct,' says Hannah, 'since they were all either dead or came down in storms.'

Upstairs are two bedrooms and a little bathroom.

Above: An expanse of white wall makes a perfect backdrop for these modern paintings, showing how the old can complement the new and vice versa.

Opposite: Cottages often have low ceilings, but using flooring that is darker than the colour of the walls gives a more spacious, unified feel.

Left: The traditional cottage look is achieved in the bedroom not through the use of frills and flowery chintzes but through the presence of solid, unfussy furniture and delicate bed hangings.

Right: On the south-facing side of the cottage is the main terrace. It's a jungle of interesting plants and containers, looking down into the garden. The carved wooden cat is by Reece Ingram.

In the latter she has used grey-veined white marble. 'You're mad,' Anthony told her. But she got her own way. 'One can't be so conservative as to disallow anything modern in an old cottage. The combination of old and new can beautiful. You just have to dare.' The half-tester bed was bought in England but the hangings were bought as old bedspreads in Amsterdam. 'They were a bit look-through so I lined them.' The windows are hung with a modern Indian fabric, lined to keep out the draughts. The original oak floorboards also warm the room by their depth of colour, but tactile warmth is provided by a soft carpet.

The house stands in the very middle of the garden. While it contains all the transitional element of the cottage garden, there is certain modern interpretation evident in the use of decking, including a hot tub. From the windows on three sides of the house one can see a pond. But step outside and you stand on timber decking running right around the cottage and beside the water. You could almost imagine yourself at sea, were it not for the overhang of a weeping willow and the umbrellas of gunnera.

Right: The garden is partly an outdoor gallery with, above, 'Two Members of the Committee' by Patricia Volk and, below, 'Two Hares' by Sophie Ryder.

Opposite: The front façade of a five-hundred-year-old timber-framed cottage, which sits between two lakes. The sculpture, 'Eclipse', is by Barry Mason.

The waterside terrace proceeds over changes of level and culminates in a vine-hung pergola under which is a hot tub, its sides concealed by planks of the same timber as the decking. Because of this, the tub, like the dog kennel and the machinery for the boiler are unobtrusive, hiding modern comforts for dog and human alike within the shell of a natural and naturally ageing material. Each plant and each pot react to create a completely satisfactory outdoor living space around the house. 'We live outside in the summer,' says Hannah. 'We have all our meals out on the terrace and do all our entertaining there. In winter the cottage is cosy and atmospheric.'

Pots furnish the terrace. They are a strong feature, not mimsy little things but massive,

planted with great ferns and hostas and the 2-
metre (6-feet) high scarlet flower spikes of
Beschorneria yuccoides. There are two other pots,
from China and glazed in deepest blue, one
containing sagittaria (arrowhead) and the other,
rushes in water. Serene among the pots, the large,
sculptural plants and the practical planking are
two large timber cats by Reece Ingram.

This is not a 'pretty' garden in the sense that
there are masses of profuse, mixed annual colour –
its planting is very carefully controlled – but the
rounded stone, the unsophisticated furniture and
the pots create the effect of random effortlessness.
These is no tension between the antique and the
contemporary. In effect, the whole creates a
perfects harmony.

TOWN STYLE

Town planning is an ancient art. The rectangular plan used for the eighth-century BC city of Magna Graecia, one of the earliest Hellenic colonies, was copied by Hippodamos in the fifth century BC for his reconstruction of the city of Miletus and for the port of Piraeus in Athens. The principles of rational town planning, expounded by Hippodamos, are based on a chequerboard grid system, which divides the town into areas for the different functions of the city.

Some form of rational planning, as opposed to allowing mere urban sprawl, was a necessity by 500 BC. The Acropolis (meaning 'upper city') had been inhabited for the last 5,000 years, but by 500 BC the population had reached approximately 100,000. Hippodamos had the advantage of the skills developed by architects of the previous century who had learnt how to cut stone and marble and replaced the brick and timber previously used for construction.

Sadly, few town-dwellers nowadays can afford to dwell in marble halls. The pressure on space and the value of building land have led to more and more infilling. Those houses that once had large gardens have smaller ones now; the remainder having been sold off for building land. Increasingly, poorer housing stock has been converted for the use of the middle classes.

Few of us want to be purist when it comes to living in a period town house. Hours spent blacking the kitchen range is not our idea of spending time in the kitchen, and central heating is easier than coal. And no matter how keen we are on D-I-Y or on calling in the decorators, we would never keep up the pace of redecoration enjoyed, for example, in London's Georgian town houses. Unlike country houses of that period, the smart town houses were continuously occupied and constantly remodelled. In those days, houses like those around Grosvenor Square, London, were owned by 'upholders', the equivalent of the modern interior designer and of similarly fashionable status. Contemporary designers are but pale reflections of the upholders, for not only did they curtain, paper, upholster, gild and carve out an interior into which London society was received, they would also design, make, transport and erect the furniture as well. They rented the houses out for the Season, after which they would arrange to let the houses on longer leases before redecorating them in the latest style in the following year.

Examples of voguish dictates can be seen in English Heritage's Architectural Study Collection. As many as eighteen papers were peeled from one wall of a house in Maddox Street, London, spanning over a century of the attentions of these dedicated followers of fashion. They begin with a hand-blocked Regency stripe, progress though various floral and rather grand crested papers until an astonishing geometric pattern appears around 1850, which, had it not had successive layers pasted on top, would have easily passed as a 1950s paper. The house must have changed owners in the 1880s, for how else is it possible to explain the restrained but wonderful sprays of roses and lilies to a foil paper of rococo leaves of a bilious yellow against an arsenic green background. Obviously it was not a great success – the next paper is a subdued pastel stripe of the watered silk variety.

Living in a period town house, then, does not mean that you should feel constrained to use bright yellow and arsenic green. It is more practical and often more intriguing to hint at the origins of the house. A modern sofa covered in a Regency stripe is both more comfortable and less expensive than the real thing.

Above right: The garden as an extension of the house – in town, the room outside, often hot and sheltered, can be a wonderful sun trap and support a range of plants that would not otherwise be possible.

Below right: A light, elegant glass roof helps to blur the distinction between inside room and conservatory, while snappy checked upholstery and an elegant chair are appropriate for the town house setting.

Using one colour for floors, walls and the sink-surround, together with the sink's clean lines, creates an apparently seamless effect in this bathroom.

Of course, where they are good, the architectural details should be preserved – shutters, plaster work, cornices, skirtings, fireplaces and door cases are all valuable – but converting the dark basement into one big kitchen and family room, lightened by glazed doors on to the garden at the back is not a crime. Leaving the wine cellar *in situ* for use as a walk-in larder as well would be inspired. The tragedy of most contemporary house builders is that they seem to have forgotten entirely about the joys of larders and laundries. Taking a slice out of a large family bathroom, for example, is a small price to pay for the luxury of being able to get the washing machine and drier out of the kitchen.

Most decorative transgressions are committed through ignorance or slavery to fashion. The mania for stripped pine, for example, has led to countless Victorian town houses being ruined by freshly stripped doors of poor quality pine that were never intended to face the world in their nakedness. Together with the woodwork to the windows, they present a depressing and darkened aspect to the rooms, hall and landings.

The small garden of a town house needs to be treated as an extension of the house, working outwards from the style of the interior. In this way, the garden becomes almost an outdoor room. And the word 'garden' should really become the term 'outdoor space'. Screens of trellis, wall or shrubs can then be used to break up its sense of confinement, and the boundary can be de-emphasized by the judicious distraction of a small tree or a large pot to provide an alternative focal point. A small garden needs to feel spacious and tranquil. It is both pretentious and counter-productive to attempt to ape the characteristics that are permitted by the wider expanses of the country garden.

The same principle applies to the roof or terrace. Furnish it with plants certainly, but do not forget that there may be restrictions on the weight that the structure will bear. Remember, too, that potted plants need regular feeding and watering. If the time you can spend on maintenance is limited, you need to decide at the outset how much time you can give to tending your plants. The other aspect of roof planting to be borne in mind is the wind – foliage that scorches easily in a cold wind should be avoided.

Colour can be used more positively in a restricted space, and this applies not only to flowers and foliage but also to the colours of painted walls and the materials used for containers. Used sensitively and with a feel for the appropriate style, you can achieve a visual unity between inside and out. Simple colour combinations can be extremely effective – silver-grey foliage with blue walls or lemon flowers with terracotta, for instance. Take your lead from the colour inside the house, particularly where glazed doors are the connecting link.

To create a strong effect, to give a feeling of space and unity, it is important to avoid cluttering the garden. Too often a simple space is spoiled by too many pots, which are too small and contain too many different colours. Add one hanging basket too many or introduce overwrought furniture and over-patterned fabric and the garden will become something at odds with a stylish interior. Outside it seems to be so easy to go haywire very quickly.

A modicum of formal furniture can be used to make town sitting rooms appear more spacious. Ruched blinds expose the window shutters, but even when they are lowered, the effect may be chilling on a cold winter's night.

The problems of heat and shade are exacerbated in the urban garden. For long periods in each day much of the garden may be in shade. Later in the day the garden can become baking hot, causing plants to pull towards the light. Generally, plants need plenty of water each day, especially where there is a lot of masonry – and that includes the wall to the garden, because the footings soak up moisture.

The conservatory is increasingly a feature of the town garden. Well planted and well ventilated, it can be a wonderful outside room. There is a fine distinction between a conservatory used in this way and one used as additional interior space. Remember that plants drop their leaves regularly, that in an artificial enclosure they are subject to more disease than outside and that they will need even more water than when outdoors. None of these features is good for upholstery. Where conservatories are built in snowier parts of the world, provision must be made for melt. In hotter climates, a pergola or loggia is a good alternative, creating a shady transitional space between the house and the outside.

Finally, lighting is one of the most important but most often overlooked considerations in the town house. These houses tend to be dark, and until recently electric lighting was fairly inflexible, confined to table lights and pendants with limited projection. Low-voltage halogen has revolutionized domestic illumination and can be extended to the garden to create a continuity of space and style.

LOFT CONVERSION

Victorian industrial architecture has only relatively recently enjoyed a good press. It came somewhat late in the day, after a good deal of it had been demolished, and when we see what good use can be made of it – as in this conversion of two brick warehouses with a river view – one could weep for all those that were destroyed in more careless times.

Good, solid brickwork, beautifully fashioned arches and mouldings, strong, elegant joinery to stout timbers – would that contemporary ware-housing, not to mention domestic housing, could be so built. By knocking together these warehouses and employing a creative imagination, a more splendid and dramatic town house has been achieved than could ever have been designed from scratch.

The overall effect combines all these qualities. It is dramatic and lofty, yet it is comfortable and warm. There are elements of the theatrical, but you are left in no doubt that real people live here. It has international undertones and a theatrical feel, yet it is rooted in 'Englishness'. The sitting room looks straight out on to the river. The bare brick walls,

although handsome with their curved mouldings and niches and buttresses, are relieved of any residual claustrophobic qualities by the light that streams through the windows, by the view, by the height of the ceilings, by the warmth of the timbers and by the rich colours and textures of all the fabrics. The rug's colours echo the ochre of the brick, and the deep russet at its centre is reflected by the apricot upholstery of two wide Chesterfields. The screen and the fender take these colours deeper still, with the screen bridging the gap between the timbers and the furniture, being at the same time in the tradition of older sitting rooms.

The dining room continues these themes. The terracotta and dark blue, the handsome mahogany and leather chairs and the inlaid drum table are in

Above: Graceful archways, reminiscent of Renaissance Italy, perfectly frame the view over the river while at the same time providing a sense of privacy.

Right: Warehouses are usually converted in modern style, but here rich colours and traditional furniture work superbly against the exposed brick.

the tradition of good houses. Placed on the island of the carpet, surrounded by the warehouse walls and a pine boarded and glass ceiling, it looks as if a piece of William IV living had appeared on a magic carpet. The classical vases and marble-topped console work well with the brick, and there is more than a hint of the classical about their combination. The surprise of the striped curtains and swagged pelmet is balanced by the angular contortions of the leafless tree. The exceptional attractiveness of this room lies in its pulling together of antique and modern, the craftsmanship of the different ages, the use of natural materials, albeit man-worked, and just enough greenery (and green leather) to set it all off.

Bare brick walls have been eschewed for the bedrooms, but beams, rugs and rich fabrics continue the unity of the reception rooms. Dramatic swags and folds of fabrics lend a voluptuous air to otherwise traditional furnishings.

The kitchen simply draws its pine ceiling down into the cupboards and housings. There is no discontinuity – the one simply flows into the other. The colouring of the floor tiles is reflected back in the colours of the walls, and the long limed refectory table, in its lightness, length and position, becomes the focal point of the room. The

Opposite above: The lessons of this kitchen in a converted warehouse could equally well apply to the conversion of agricultural buildings in the country.

Opposite right: The dining room is a perfect example of the way in which the themes of drama, tradition and comfort are pursed. This juxtaposition of sophisticated furniture and fabrics with raw brick is a *tour de force*.

Opposite below: Even though the brick has been covered, the bedroom echoes the treatment of the other rooms of the conversion with its use of rich, luxurious fabrics and colour.

Right: Underneath the arches is an elegant conservatory. Notice how the door and windows maintain the architectural detail of the original. The solid timber furniture is used to create an unfussy look and echoes the timber boarding of the ceiling, thereby drawing attention to the arches.

director's chairs, which are fitted with embossed leather, are more durable versions of those used by the late owner for most of his working life.

The interior moves outside with little change of pace or style. The arches that now frame the garden terrace are repetitions of the arches in the interior and of those that now make the

conservatory between them. Such a room provides a welcome transition when it is too cold or wet to be outside, but its styling and treatment is as vigorous as the terrace itself – the same stone flooring, the same timber seating and the same raw brickwork. The unity between the interior of the house, between conservatory and terrace is

inescapable. There is also a straightforwardness about the whole that totally lacks pretension.

A very early concept of a garden space was that it should provide protection – from one's enemies probably at first, but also from the elements – for plants provide support and comfort to the beings in their midst. Imagine this terrace with no greenery and it would be monastic in its austerity. Treated formally it would become an artwork; treated casually it invites participation and relaxation.

The views from the terrace and of and from the backdrop of its arched boundary walls are fairly spectacular. Anything less than the scale here achieved would appear mere frippery. Imagine how distracting and out of place would be hanging baskets in the arches and window boxes along the railings and a few uninviting, white aluminium chairs.

By creating bold groupings of mixed vegetation the arches are softened though not weakened. All the plants are contained in large terracotta pots and by grouping the major ones together, watering by drip irrigation is made far easier. The colouring is clever: it mixes fresh green and blue-green and greys from the soft round blue-green of a tall *Eucalyptus gunnii* (which, if one might suggest, is slightly too tall and will need some hard pruning shortly to make it multi-stemmed) to the sprays of grey helichrysum and the deep blue-grey of artemisia trailing on the floor. The frondy gold leaflets of *Gleditsia triacanthos* 'Sunburst' looks well against the brickwork arches, and this is a good choice for this exposed position because it can stand an amount of drought. A simple pot of the yellow-tipped scarlet daisy, *Gaillardia artistata*, is the only significant flower colour on the terrace. Less is definitely more.

Above: An interesting small detail is the collection of herbs on the table. These, and the candlestick, lend a touch of domesticity to the scene.

Left: The architecture is chunky, the view is huge and exciting and both plant grouping and garden furniture need to be in scale with their surroundings to create a unified and positive ambience. Even the cat seems happy.

The spiky architectural plant on the other side of the arch is *Cordyline australis*, which moves to the conservatory in winter because it does not appreciate a cold wind. The ivy in the oil jar beside it is quite hardy, however, and like the evergreen eucalyptus provides some winter interest.

The centrepiece is created by the table with its collection of herbs, and when the simple umbrella is up, even more of a focal point is made. Candlelit at night, the view must be magical. Underlying the

relationship between the terrace, conservatory and interior is the emphasis on freedom of movement in and out of the building, and even where this is not possible, the eye still sees the space outside through carefully sited glass, preserving the interdependence of house and garden. The internal drama of the house itself, with its height and the excitement of its architecture is an echo of the excitement of the view from the terrace and the drama of the old brick arches. There is a freedom both inside and outside, which is rare in town and the whole of this property both uses and creates it.

MINIMALIST TOWN HOUSE

Here is a brick-built Victorian terraced house in town. It has sliding-sash, bay windows to the basement and ground floor, a bit of fancy brickwork, a slate roof and a narrow front door within the open brick porch. There is nothing in particular to recommend it. Walk up the narrow path and up seven steps to the front door. Close your eyes and take the last step up into the house. Now open your eyes. You are standing in a rectangular, space-age womb of white, your only link to old-fashioned forms of human sustenance are the long pine table and benches on a wide-planked pine floor.

The transformation was effected by John Pawson. He kept the shell and principal structure of an urban late-Victorian terraced house and turned the interior over to a modern treatment. He removed the cornices, the dado rails, the tiled fireplaces, the balusters and newel posts, and a few non-load-bearing walls, together with the aspidistra and antimacassars, and took the house, with apparently hardly a kick or a scream, into the minimalist world of the twentieth century.

For a start, he did away with the long, narrow hall. The dividing wall between the front parlour and the hall has been removed, as far as structural support would allow. On the left, the steep narrow staircase rises unembellished between plain square white walls. On the right, the front parlour and the back room have been knocked together to yield one white open space on a pine ground. The fireplace is still there, but it has become a square hole in a solid white rectilinear chimney breast, raised to a level that permits seating alongside its length. The centre of the room is taken up with the two wide pine planks, which form a modern trestle table. The bottom third of the window – notice that the sliding-sash appearance of the window has been retained – is taken up with an unobtrusive

Above: This terrace house is typical of thousands of urban British homes. The kitchen was often at garden level at the rear, with living accommodation on the ground floor.

Left: Simple rectilinear space broken by twisted stems in a round vase can be very tranquil.

radiator. There are no sliding patio doors here, so in a sense the architectural integrity, or what remains of it (because it has been reduced to its minimum), has been retained. It is only the detail that has been shelved.

And ingeniously so. Behind the slabs of white fascia panels on the left-hand wall lurk all the storage facilities once supplied by dressers, chests of drawers and sideboards. There are no doors other than these downstairs. The two rectangular

openings at the end of the room are for the window and entrance to the kitchen. Galley-shaped, its path is dictated by the continuation of the wide pine floorboards so that the eye runs right through, either to the window at the end of

Above: The galley kitchen feels light and pleasant, despite its width. The light from the window is supplemented by artificial light, the fitments for which are hidden behind the reveals along the right-hand side.

Opposite: The only decoration in this room is provided by the vertical and horizontal lines, further emphasized by the division of the table along its length and by the parallel lines of the floorboards and bench and table edges.

Left: The tomb-like stairwell is completely unadorned; nothing is allowed on the walls and the treads are bare boards.

Above: The floorboards have been extended to form the bed-head, maintaining the horizontal lines seen elsewhere. Built-in cupboards ensure that no clutter is visible.

Left: The homage to rectilinearity is continued in the bathroom, with the sarcophagus bath, large, plain window and built-in bench.

the main room or to the end of the kitchen. There are no distractions here either. The eye is not taken by overhead cupboards, but instead runs parallel with the marble work surfaces, into which the hob and sink are inset, straight through to the wide window overlooking the garden at its end.

There is no let-up on the theme. Upstairs, the pattern of white and pine is repeated. A horizontal pine headboard falls in with the line of the pine floorboards and the pattern of rectangular white fascia boards for doors to storage replicates those downstairs. Your book at bedtime and the alarm clock, though, have to go on the floor. The bathroom is even more uncompromising: bath,

same rectangular template as the interior – the long concrete outdoor table, the squared lattice trellising – plants do not grow in rectangles. Nature is curved and the fecund shapes of her leaves and her flowers is the more impressive set against the hard shapes of man-made structures.

The small garden at the rear of this town house is below ground level, and although the garden is walled to approximately 1.5 metres (5 feet) high, from the living level neighbouring gardens were all too obvious. A fine squared lattice has been used to raise the enclosure height along the rear of the garden, therefore, and this was quickly covered by the planted wisteria. A fig shows its curves nearer

Above: At the end of the kitchen a plate-glass window allows an unimpeded view into 'the garden'.

Right: Fine trellis creates a sense of enclosure in 'the garden' and acts as a foil to the bold leaves of the *Magnolia grandiflora.*

floor, seating, is all rectangular, cold, marbleized. It is also very clever. The lavatory is probably the only thing in the house that isn't rectangular. But the bathroom does summarize the reductionism of the house. If you ever thought it might be possible to reduce architecture, artefacts and furniture to two- or three-dimensional rectangles, this is your model.

The plate glass window at the end of the kitchen is designed to fudge the question of what is outside, what is inside. At this point man-made construction defers to nature. Although all the constructs in the room outside are built to the

the house, where the contrast between its sensuous nature and the rectilinear geometry of the interior can be appreciated.

The garden itself has been treated as a room and is almost entirely paved in the same terrazzo as the table running across it. Behind it is a mix of green and grey herbs – including thyme and sage – and it

The central part of the garden has been raised to get more light, and planting is, therefore, contained around the edges.

is dominated by a standard *Magnolia grandiflora*, whose lush globes of flower are thrown into relief by the right angles of every thing that surrounds it.

It is a fallacy to suppose that everyone who has an outside space enjoys gardening. The space comes with the house, and many feel obliged to do something with it. Such a treatment as this is clean and crisp throughout the year, and it can be swept and hosed down. The look goes with the house and its interior by providing the few minimal curves and the antithesis of nature in a highly controlled setting. One might argue whether such a modern treatment in such an urban location is not always entirely appropriate.

LISBON COURTYARD HOUSE

Throughout this book we look at period, location, style and intention, and the ways in which it is possible to integrate 'in with out' to achieve some sort of total environment for the people who live in it and use it. In this example, a Portuguese town house, a definite feeling for the design of the interior has not been entirely carried through to the outside.

The interior has been arranged for dramatic effect on three principles: old and new, tri-colour schemes and unity. It mixes antique furniture and paintings with modern furniture, lights and ornaments; it uses black, white and red as the main colours for walls, floors and fabrics, and it keeps to these combinations of old and new, colour scheme and pattern throughout.

The floor throughout is of white ceramic tiles with black diamond insets, apart from the stairs, which are carpeted in red with a gold and red chequered border, which repeats the chequered theme of the tiles and echoes the red of the curtain fabric while picking up the gold of the gilded

mirror and picture frames. Even the treatment of the staircase reflects the other themes of the house – the vertical lines of the turned baluster are painted white, while the horizontal and diagonal lines of the rail are painted black, echoing the stripes and black and white scheme used elsewhere.

The balance of old and new and the colour scheme of red and black against white, with gilt trimming, is adhered to rigidly. Broad black and white checks are used to upholster the modern sofa with cushions and throws of red and white and black and white. A comparatively modern adjustable armchair, cushioned in modern black and white stripes, faces an antique armchair, traditionally upholstered in red brocade. Even the portraits and shields are red, black and gold.

Above: The colours used in the entrance hall are repeated in the upholstery fabric of the garden chairs on the terrace. This is a simple way to create a sense of continuity.

Right: The strong colours are offset and unified by the plain white walls and black and white tiled floor that are used throughout the house.

Right: Even the staircase and landing are decorated to sustain the colour scheme that is used elsewhere.

Opposite above: Repetition of detail in stripes and in colours is used in every room, but each room – here the sitting room – retains its own individuality.

Opposite below left: The galleried landing, with its bold black and white fabrics, doubles as a spare bedroom

Opposite below right: The green and gilt armoire introduces a new colour to the furnishing of the main bedroom, but even here the black, white and red seen in the other rooms dominates.

Where there is a departure from this scheme – as with the leopard-skin pouffe – it is repeated elsewhere in subtle ways – the leopard-skin cushion on the day-bed and the leopard-skin effect to the frames of the drawing on the walls, or, more obviously, with the upholstery on the ottoman in the main bedroom.

Only in the bedroom is another colour permitted, thereby softening, without losing sight of, the black, white and red scheme. The avocado green and gilt painted armoire and bedsteads are typically Portuguese pieces. Had they been painted red or black or white, the effect would have been even more overpowering and inappropriate to the setting of a bedroom.

By using simple stripes and dramatic colours, this

house presents a bold and striking effect that nevertheless allows for the introduction of a variety of elaborate pieces of furniture. Apart from the Portuguese armoire and bedsteads, the bedroom also contains a French gilded console table, an ebonized and gilded display table, a French Empire armchair, a pouffe with a needlework top, and a chest of drawers on which a *trompe l'œil* scene has been painted.

Unless there is a plain and unifying background – in this case, white walls and ceilings and a black and white floor – it would be difficult to integrate elaborate pieces without losing the drama of the overall effect. The background also makes a clean canvas on which to paint the broad brush strokes of colour. By working with three basic bold

Left: Inside or out? It is difficult to tell.

Right: There is a decaying charm to the rear courtyard of this Lisbon house. *Cyperus,* ferns, ivy and the gentle drip of water have all been used to create a grotto-like retreat which is cool and inviting in summer.

rightly in Britain as 'crazy paving'. A plain brushed-concrete infill between a linear pattern might more successfully have reflected the proportions of the house and echoed its strong linear decoration.

When it comes to furniture in such a setting, where the ground area is limited but the ceiling is endless, bold and simple lines generally work well. Here, where the principles that guided the interior might have been applied to good effect, the mixture of marble, iron, stone and wickerwork, confuse the eye and do not cohere to make a pleasing whole. We have seen in other houses how a clutter can be composed into a handsome grouping. A concentration on a few simple, strong forms within a limited area can often given the illusion of space, while providing a sympathetic and harmonious partner to the house.

TURN-OF-THE-CENTURY HOUSE

The conversion of this London house has been undertaken in a witty and expansive style. The wit lies in the translation to a modern idiom of hints and pointers to the house's Victorian origins. These subtleties must be searched out for they are not immediately obvious. What is immediately striking, however, is its expansiveness – there are big flowers in big pots, big plants, big pictures, big busts – but the size is deceptive. In fact, everything has been done to enlarge its proportions.

In the master bedroom one wall has been exposed. The appearance of London stock brick gives a solid edge to the room, providing a strong and distinctive feel and a reminder of the house's age in a room that has otherwise all the muted harmonies of contemporary decoration – walls and ceiling in the same cream, fitted self-coloured carpet and discreet but powerful low-voltage lighting (which is, in fact, used throughout).

The solidity is picked up again in the use of sturdy mahogany tables, with marble tops, a foil for the collections of large pieces of blue and white china. On the wall on either side of the bed hang two much older pier glasses in gilded frames with painted panels, against which the shining steel of the four-poster makes an amusing juxtaposition. The dimensions of the room have been increased by using double doors. Double doors generally have this effect, but here, because space is limited, they are folding.

The main reception room downstairs has been created by knocking through to make one large room. At one end is the fireplace, the surround of restrained stone with a classical yet contemporary feel. The recesses on either side of the chimney breast have been mirrored entirely, increasing the reflection of light and adding a further dimension of depth. The bay window retains the original form of the windows – sliding sash – and, like the fire

Above: Using mirrors in this town house conversion creates the illusion of space.

Right: The mix of contemporary lighting, fitted carpets and minimalist four-poster bed makes an unobtrusive setting for period pieces.

surround, they have been given a plain, unfussy, curtain treatment of straight, stone-coloured pleats. The floor has been left as boards. Like the cornice in this room and the exposed brick in the bedroom, they are direct glimpses of the old fabric of the house.

At the other end of the room is a comfortable contemporary sofa, dominated by the image of ancient India above. This, together with the Buddha and some other objects, lends an international feel to the room. Note again the use of solid marble tabletops. This is a design for a house based on general unifying principles, picked up again in the details.

The recurrent themes of an Indian interest in a period town setting are reiterated in the basement room. Again, spaciousness has been created by knocking rooms together – one large room being preferable to two poky ones. The bay window, just below street level, is one of the few examples where paint stripping works. In this case, the pine is of good quality, and it has been matched by the contemporary pine casing to the window-seat sofa. Building in the sofa in this way has given the room even more space. No possible form of free-standing piece could ever achieve the same effect. It also has the advantage of providing storage space, always at a premium in town houses, in the area under the seat.

Again in this room we notice the recurrent Indian theme, hinted at in the stylized paisley fabrics and the wallpaper. At the same time, it meshes well with the Staffordshire pottery, the reappearance of blue and white in the collection of meat plates on the wall, allusions to the period of the house, and the same solid, leather-upholstered dining chairs used also in the more formal setting upstairs.

The link between inside and out is provided by the conservatory. Of contemporary construction, it provides reflections of interior themes. The busts are there on the marble side-table, the floor is of the same colour as the timber floorboards on the ground floor, but here they are converted to ceramic tiling, and nuances of the East are given in

Opposite above:
The window-seat built into the bay is a comfortable and elegant way of using the available space to the best possible effect, while the use of the same fabric for the upholstery, blinds and wall covering gives the room a harmonious feel.

Opposite below:
The thoughtful use of strong colour – in the portraits, upholstery and tablecloth – provides both warmth and drama and gives the room a richness it would not otherwise have.

Right: The dining area/conservatory has been designed to accommodate – and requires – big, high foliage. This room demonstrates very well the balanced inside-outside character of this kind of extension, which, while modern compared with the rest of the house, uses fabrics and traditional furniture that maintain the period feel.

the use of bamboo and fig plants. Even the table setting picks up some of the influences of the more formal arrangements inside, but here is given a more relaxed, informal treatment, emphasized by the use of slatted timber chairs in restrained wrought iron frames.

This garden is principally a green oasis in an urban setting. Just as there are massive flower and plant displays in the house, so the garden throws together all sorts of greenery – it is primarily a foliage garden – in a joyful, verdant chaos. It masses and jostles old urns and ivies with a variety

Right: Although it is not a large garden, the space is further divided into rooms. Outside the conservatory is a paved terrace for eating outside. Because the garden is so shaded, box is used to create an all-year-round skeleton of greenery.

Below right: The hankering for grandeur is a curious phenomenon – often characterized by the urn. In this case, it is a pleasing contrast with the tulips.

Opposite: There is a lot happening in this town garden, shaded by an old cherry tree, to create a lived-in look. The owner obviously loves pottering in the garden, and it shows to advantage.

of leaf forms and textures within a comparatively small scale. The terracotta pots of box are used to punctuate an otherwise loose arrangement of plants, which allows for a huge range of interest, and this controls the overall look. It could almost be regarded as a sort of smart cottage garden, shape on shape, but arranged with a knowing eye.

The escape from the careful, structured design inside the house to the verdant sprawl of nature is staggered by the transition through the conservatory, out on to a wide, stone-paved path, which doubles as terrace, filled with terracotta pots, some filled with the evergreen box, an excellent all-year subject, and some for seasonal plants, such as tulips for late spring and petunias for summer. Most of the flowers are kept within this area nearer to the house. White-painted slatted benches and an old, weathered timber bench are surrounded by roses and petunias, and a fine old rosemary grows between urns of fern and helichrysum, all under the shade of an old *Prunus*.

Deeper into the garden a laurel, trimmed to mop-head proportions, and angelica, set against an obelisk, dominate the greenery underneath. Where there are flowers they are of restrained colours – white foxgloves, pale and dark blue delphiniums, white lupins and little clumps of forget-me-nots. As the garden progresses, climbing 'Iceberg' roses, white daisies, blue and white campanulas and deep pink foxgloves appear in front of the screen of holly and dark green, stained, slatted wood structures. These, together with the timber pyramids, stained the same dark green, threaded with glossy ivies and offset by the gold variegated leaf of *Elaeagnus pungens* 'Maculata', are reminders of a human presence, a designing hand in the apparently artless ways of nature.

This is an ideal solution for a town garden, because the interest is held within the centre of the site. In so many gardens the interest is pushed to the sides, like chairs around the parish hall. Try this look and get it wrong, however, and you have a mess. That is why the box in pots are so good – they steady the exuberance of the remainder.

MODERN STYLE

Modern in the sense of recent or contemporary embraces everything that we are building now or have been building in the recent past. This means that the term includes everything, from the energy-efficient houses that are built underground, through council houses, to villages of the kind that are planned for Poundbury, Dorset. It means supermarkets that are built to look like barns, department stores that resemble pagodas and art galleries that look like glass houses; but it also means glass houses or conservatories used as Victoriana and real barns that are converted for houses.

Often, however, when we use the term modern we take it to refer to those styles of architecture influenced by the Modern Movement, especially by Walter Gropius and Mies van der Rohe of the Bauhaus, which was optimistically established to combine 'imaginative design with technical proficiency' and produced the vast egg-box structures of steel and glass, by Le Corbusier, past master of the art of reinforced concrete, and by Frank Lloyd Wright, who set out to define the American house.

The expression of these influences is to be found in the tower blocks of housing estates and city offices, but the expression of the best of these same influences is another matter. This is where the sculptural qualities of the building are emphasized, where clean lines are pronounced, and where the use of vast stretches of glass enables the building to adopt its setting as a part of itself, much as the ancient art of Japanese gardens relied on the principle of *shakkei* (borrowed landscape). And indeed, a Japanese garden complements this style of architecture because the lines are pure, and the space is uncluttered and tranquil.

The principles to be followed in decorating houses of this sort revolve around the purity of line and colour. Using pale colours, creams and whites throughout a house will emphasize its unity. Such colours contrast well with a plain carpet, dark or light,

or rich timber flooring, or stone, tile or marble, and they will make a good foil for large pictures or sculptures. Houses like these are usually endowed with invisible storage. Shelves, cupboards and drawers lurk behind fascias and baffleboards that appear to be integral to the walls. If this is so, well and good. It means that importing chests of drawers, wardrobes, bureaux and so on will be unnecessary and much greater attention can be both paid and drawn to furniture, like couches, sofas, chairs, tables and beds, whose only purpose is the positioning of human bodies. This means that the wardrobe, chest of drawers, dressing table can all be dispensed with, leaving the bedroom with a bed and maybe a couple of armchairs and looking far more spacious.

It is a mistake to think that a modern house must have modern furniture. The pleasure of uncluttered sculptural spaces means that an antique piece can be displayed to its best advantage, that it will be picked out and that the elegance of its own lines and the quality of its craftsmanship will be complemented by the clean lines and intelligence employed in the architectural construction.

As time has gone on, 'modern' must now include that branch of architecture that employs natural materials from renewable resources. John Makepeace, the furniture maker, has built his school and manufactory entirely of timber thinnings, while inside his students make chairs and tables of the same young wood. The same thing is happening on the continent of Europe in the landscaping of public gardens, open spaces and

Above right: Like a well-tailored garment, this Australian courtyard, designed by Glenn Murcutt, has wonderful style. There is a minimalism about it, although there is enough greenery, sky and water to make an entirely satisfying composition of building with landscape.

Below right: Restraint and clean, simple lines make a light, airy backdrop for the focus of the room – the paintings. Continuity of the room with outside is achieved by transforming the flooring into decking.

The walk from bedroom to bathroom is made more interesting by the stripy runner, which echoes the lines of the louvred doors.

tracts of land beside motorways. Here they are encouraging swathes of indigenous wilder plants, such as gorses and grasses, which make good ground cover, so that the expense of maintenance will be reduced and at the same time their use as habitats, feeding and breeding grounds for all manner of wildlife will be increased.

The same goes for the garden. It is a mistake to think that the garden to a modern house must be filled with exotic plants – unless, of course, the house is situated in an exotic climate. For visual excitement we look to

Australia, South Africa, North and South America. There is a breadth and spaciousness there, combined with a belief that anything can be done with buildings and the gardens that surround them. This is where exotic gardening is done best. Japanese gardens can be made of native plants, stones and water. They do not depend for their effect on the use of exotica. Alternatively, a modern garden can be made on principles deriving from classic gardening. Wide, shallow stone steps, a green lawn and a couple of sculptured yews may be all that a modern house in a town requires.

Certainly a cottage garden would make a highly inappropriate setting for a house of glass and steel. But just as the greening of the spaces surrounding industrial areas and motorways is becoming more urgent, we must replace what we took away when we turned to agricultural monoculture – rooting up hedgerows to create bigger fields, and poisoning ourselves and the wildlife with toxic sprays – so that the sum total of all our gardens can be seen as a huge wildlife sanctuary. A natural gardening approach to the garden of a modern house has more than a few merits.

Increased global warming, with the possibility of longer periods of drought or extremes of weather conditions, is suffici``ent to encourage a move away from the garden that is based on borders filled with perennial plants. Their flowering is too short and their maintenance too time consuming. Abandoning the regime of the border- and bed-based garden also means escaping from the tyranny of clipping, cutting, lopping and mowing. Add to that the romance of meadow wildflowers and the ecological satisfaction you will undoubtedly feel when, from behind your plate-glass window, you are able to watch the teeming wildlife, and the argument for a natural garden with the modern house is nearly overwhelming.

Today's modern gardens look towards clarity and simplicity, where hard landscaping plays as dominant a role as any planting. Ornaments are no longer, perhaps, grey stone 'classical' figures or crafted terra-cotta pots. Instead, they are abstract shapes with sleek lines created from shiny materials and painted in bright colours. The effect is open, clean and ordered.

The lines of this house (also seen below) are clearly contemporary, and its clear internal spaces link through sliding doors to the deck outside. 'In' is further linked with 'out' by the use of bay trees in pots.

Inside, the chunky, modern sofas complement the solid beams and timber supports, but the gentle curve of the roof timbers prevents the space from being too cuboid.

CONTEMPORARY NEW ZEALAND HOUSE

This contemporary New Zealand house, over-hanging the sea, is the fruit of a collaboration between Simon Cornal, the architect, and Ted Smyth, a landscape designer. Together they have created a superb example of the principle of unity, not only between house and garden, but also, as importantly, between house and garden and setting. The inspiration that drives the landscape and enfolds the house, is the setting itself, the sea. The combination of house and garden is really quite breathtaking, for not only is the view superb, but so are the planes of landscape and garden treatment, receding step-by-step through the glazing of the house right into its very core.

A rectilinear U-shape, the house has two flanking wings, culminating in steep, stylized gables, with a double-height atrium on each side. From the outside looking towards the house, the thrusting gables and atria are its focal points. From the inside, however, and this is the brilliance of its dual conception, it is the landscape beyond or through the atria that is the focal point, if not the whole point of the house.

The facing interior sides of the wings have been colonnaded, a theme to be repeated inside the house. Spanning the bridge is the master bedroom, the curve of the roof above its wholly glass front reflected in the curve of the balcony. This both breaks and unites the angularity of the gables and at the same time hints at another theme we discover inside.

The interior of the house is a celebration of the house's position, glorying in its vistas. Nothing in this house could look quite so good or have as much meaning or impact if it were situated else-where. This is because the house gets its colours from the sea.

The drawing room and dining room, divided by columns, are set on a blue ground. They are

Above: The design for this contemporary New Zealand home demonstrates the potential of inside-outside living.

Left: The perfection of this room is that it has been designed wholly for its setting. The glass apse, which is repeated in the parallel wing, is its glory.

The unified style of the interior depends on the use of blue and white with touches of a third colour – green in the sitting room (below), turquoise in the dining room (far right) and rose red in the bedroom (bottom). Even the long passage (right) maintains the blue theme with pictures and a splendid vase.

Right: Below the atrium the swimming pool is only an echo of the sea beyond. The picture is framed and held by two superb trees.

Left: Airy elegance overlooking the sea is achieved with minimal metal supports for the apse, so that as little as possible detracts from its setting.

separated only along the length of the colonnades when you glimpse the grey ceramic tiles underneath. In the drawing room between the sofas the blue ground is overlaid by a deeper blue rug, the deep blue of antique Chinese silk carpets. And the focal point of the dining room, of course, is the picture above the fireplace of the house itself. These rooms subtly mix the colours of the moods of the sea – its white spray, its shivering grey, the graduated blue of its shifting depths, black when it is murderous. Even the water in the small pool behind the dining table has been given the same hues, by using a dark lining and border. Liquid and solid appear continuous. You could almost be afloat.

And this is a theme that is hinted at by the columns, by the curve of the bedroom roof, by the style of the fireplaces, by the curved cupboard between the fireplace and the window, by the use of chrome to the skirtings and for the fire irons, by ebonized chairs, mantelshelf, and matching curved cupboard. They are all details evocative of the ocean liners of the 1930s. It is extremely subtle but it is there. The bedroom picks up the same theme, with the shape of the window and curtains, the deckrails to the curved balcony outside and the vaulted roof. The basket-work chair is not Lloyd Loom, but it could as well have been.

The other gabled wing is a less formal sitting room with simply varnished floorboards and white on white for the furniture and walls. Despite the comparative lack of formality in this room, the atrium at its apex lends it a cathedral-like quality. This room is all about light, hence there is very little colour save for the timber ground. It takes its depth from the grey-blue paving outside so that the whole room is all of a piece with its landscape.

Ted Smyth describes himself as a landscape artist.

Above: Drama comes from the reflections of blue in the black-tiled swimming pool, itself a bridge between the dining room one the side and the garden on the other.

Above right: Where there are sea views, there is usually wind, and to counteract this, a generously planted internal courtyard also leads to the front door.

Below right: Strong subtropical foliage forms a contrast with blue lattice work, moss and boulders in the internal courtyard.

He began as an artist and moved his talents to a broader canvas. He has achieved a sculptural quality on a grand scale here by playing with the shifting planes of landscape and seascape, with the level moving in both directions from outside through the glazing into the house, and back again to outside. To describe the composition as 'slick' sounds ingenuous, but the fine detail and sensitivity to construction, planting and manipulation of the planes of sight create a glamour and precision seldom seen, except perhaps in old movies – and there you have again hints of the 1930s ocean liners.

Smyth prefers using materials that he calls anonymous – they are in no way natural. He prefers ceramic tiles or even stainless steel for his surfaces: weathered timber is of no interest and his water features are never like natural watercourses. He believes that: 'An artist should have a personal vocabulary which he or she will always be developing, and while the physical content may

vary and the focus of the garden be onward or outwards towards a deeper landscape beyond, there should be an underlying continuity of structural elements in colour and plant material.' This structure rides above its seascape exactly as a luxury liner, the curve and swell of its terraces simulating the rhythms of the sea. The scale and colour of the pool in the middle distance works with the infinity of the horizon, together with the

Although they are not visible from the atrium, there are terraces beneath the swimming pool and a last look-out terrace. The swimming pool, which is of the overflow type, has a very precise, sharp edge.

infinity lent to the swimming pool, by depriving it of the definition of edges to create the most dramatic of connections.

Looking back to the house, the pool steps up to a grey ceramic tile surround and terrace. Note the scale of the pool. The terrace and the height of the eaves all have a proportionate relationship. The plants and the furniture are the only decoration in a very controlled relationship.

Few designs for landscape or architecture exhibit quite so much discipline and control nor such creativity of shared vision as the realization of this composition. The plants, the colour scheme, the pieces of furniture have nothing to do with it. Its success is, rather, to do with the overall unity of the grander scales of architecture, landscape and setting. This represents the best of the legacy of Modernism.

MODERNIST DESIGN

Modernism has taken something of a battering of late, but younger designers have increasingly come to appreciate how its concepts and principles questioned the classical idiom that traditionalists hold so dear.

Comparatively few domestic Modernist buildings were designed, and even fewer built, in Britain before the advent of the Second World War. That fact, combined with an obsession for the Arts & Crafts movement, probably accounts for a general reluctance in the public attitude to acceptance of this alternative new way.

One of the few Modernist houses to be built in Britain was designed by the architect Patrick Gwynne for himself and his parents in 1937. Today, The Homewood, with its flat roofs, white

Above: The horizontal line of The Homewood, built in 1937, contrasts beautifully with the vertical pine and silver birch trees in whose Surrey midst it sits.

Right: The furniture, hangings, picture windows and minimal cornicing of the living room illustrate all the architectural and design features of Modernism.

Above: In the kitchen the sleek lines of the charcoal grey cupboards combine with the overhanging traditional *batterie de cuisine*.

Right: The mix of curved wall and glazing bars of the glass inside and brick piers outside emphasizes the vertical lines of the building, which parallel the trees that surround the house.

façades and bands of horizontal glazing contrasting with the vertical trunks of pine and birch from the landscape of an older garden on the site, looks as crisp and exciting as it did when it was finally completed in 1939. The National Trust so highly regards the architectural quality of this house that it has decided to buy it, keeping much of the original contents.

This is Patrick Gwynne's spiral staircase seen from above. Given its ocular form, the addition of a 'pupil' on the tiled floor below is an amusing detail.

The original shock effect of The Homewood is still there as you approach it at the end of a long wooded drive. The main living room is on the first floor so life is conducted among the tree tops. It is a reminder of the influences of Le Corbusier's Villa Savoye at Poissy-sur-Seine, France; Philip Johnson's joy in nature, realized in his Glass House at New Canaan, Connecticut, which was set among wooded park land; and Frank Lloyd's Wright Prairie Houses at Oak Park and Riverside, Chicago, whose terraces merged with the gardens, or Fallingwater, Pennsylvania.

This room is spacious, light and airy. It has a remarkably quiet feel, for nothing obtrudes on its architectural qualities. All the lines of this room are straight and clean. Polished narrow pine

While the terrace and decking and railings that run around the outside are rectilinear – straight horizontal and vertical lines and crosshatching – the outdoor chairs and table are curved. It is as if the house were saying that although architecture is formal and is based on Euclidean geometry, people and their lives are not.

The elegant spiral staircase is typical of its period. Like the decking outside, it reflects the vaguely nautical air of much 1930s architecture. The staircase itself would have made a grand set for a Busby Berkeley musical.

Downstairs the simplicity of the interior verticals reflects those of the exterior, with the lines of the brick piers outside marrying with the black glazing bars. Notice, too, the subtlety of the colours and the way in which the two curved walls (which achieve their effect precisely because they are curved, in contradistinction to all the other straight lines) appear as cream folds between a tiled white floor and a white ceiling.

The flavour of the kitchen is timelessly modern. There is nothing about it that speaks of the decade in which it was designed in the definitive way in which the staircase speaks of its era. Apart from the rather outdated cooker hood and electrical sockets, this could be a kitchen built in the 1970s or 1990s. Charcoal grey, white and chocolate brown emphasize the handsome, no-nonsense lines but do not take minimalism to extremes. There are plenty of hanging rails for the cooking utensils, and the gleam of copper adds the warmth of purpose of real life, reminders that the inhabitants actually cook and eat.

floorboards run its length horizontally following the horizontal glazing bars, while the verticals are echoed by the folding Japanese screen doors and the long, simple pleats of the hangings. The colours are all neutral: a cream ceiling, which picks up a depth of colour reflected off the pine floor, mustard hangings and ivory rugs. Only the furniture – and then only some of the furniture – has curves as if to emphasize the sensuous, the relaxing and the tranquil. Two reclining chairs of the period, one black leather, one cream, epitomize this feel. In the adjoining room a circular, smoked glass-topped dining table picks up the curves of an antique grand piano.

Above left: A deck at the end of the long sitting room links down to the plunge pool and entertainment terrace beneath the house.

Left: A cantilevered terrace in concrete hangs out over the garden.

The vertical form of the brick pilotis on which the house sits echoes the stems of the silver birch trees into which the main living room looks. The clarity of the design is very appealing.

While the house appears to be a sculptural composition within its treed landscape, not unlike a Palladian mansion within its park, it is, in fact, totally integrated within it, both physically, by the overhanging first floor, and visually, by the use of so much glass. Elevating such a house on columns, or pilotis, provides a useful area in a north European climate for an entrance and car parking beneath the living space. At The Homewood, at the rear of the house, the arrangement gives entertainment space, for there is a covered terrace linked to a plunge pool. This can be approached at ground level or down an open staircase from the deck terrace at the end of the living space above.

The pool surround and terrace are all paved with the same pre-cast concrete slabs. On either side of steps leading down into the pool there are small decorative ponds, which, when full with plants appreciative of moisture, act as a light screen to the main pool. Under the overhang is a bar and a dining space, ideal for those warm summer evenings when a dew suddenly descends.

The logic of this house and its setting, the marriage between its function and aesthetic within the framework of total integration which offers scope at the same time as providing a discipline, has surely to be a vindication of Modernism for the most die-hard traditionalist.

CARIBBEAN STAGE-SET

Here is a house that combines inside and out beautifully. It embodies the best virtues of modern style with a dignity and simplicity that derive from the classical. It is both timeless and exciting. If you thought that it must have been designed by someone used to evoking flavours, feels and moods through subtle hints, while at the same time interpreting those nuances in the modern idiom, you would be right. This house on Barbados, along with several others on the island, was built in 1969 by the late Oliver Messel, the British set designer, who had the taste of a gentleman, the imagination of an artist and the rational intelligence of an historian and scientist combined.

Constructed of pale coral stone, set in a tropical though verdant garden overlooking the sea, the house is a wide and generous backdrop of restrained elegance for the exits and the entrances of its inhabitants. Just as the set in the theatre must not swamp or dwarf or upstage the play or its actors, so this house has been designed to yield to the lives of its owners, the players.

It is also very much an inside-outside house. Wide galleries and shaded cloisters link the spaces inside with those outside. The entry loggia, columned on one side and shuttered on the other with a fretwork gate to the garden, could as well be external as internal. This exercise in parallel identity is completed by the use of identical ferns between each column. The strong lines of the building are contrasted with exotic leaf forms and shapes, with the deep blue of the sea beyond. It is a modern composition because it is linear – building, line, furniture lines and leaf all form balance – but there is more than a hint of the classical and the cathedral in its columns. Where so much modern architecture feels uncomfortable because it is so uncompromising, overriding the needs and expression of people in a misguided

Above: This lush property in Barbados has a double colonnaded pink façade.

Right: The generous arches around the loggia make this a perfect example of inside-outside space – a dining area that opens directly onto the terrace.

The references in this portico are both classical (the columns) and Moorish (the curved lattice gates). This is the entrance to the house, and the inside–outside flavour is conveyed by the sophisticated tiling and columns.

homage to art for art's sake or searing those needs in the white heat of technology, the balance here is superb. The materials are all natural and induce no space-age anomie.

From the main loggia at the back of the house, which is used as an inside-outside drawing room and dining room, an abundance of wide arches open directly on to the surrounding terraces and garden. The juncture is seamless. Only discreet changes of level and a slight alteration in the

flooring material define the separation between different areas. This continuity is achieved by a number of intelligent architectural devices.

The walls remain rough so that you can see the mortar between the blocks, although they have been all painted a warm sand. The terrazzo floor of mushroom-pink and stone diamonds, with black-green marble insets, is, in contrast, a highly polished and sophisticated material, as suitable for an interior as it is for the exterior. The stone cornice is carried

Tables, chairs, sofas and chandeliers usually furnish interiors, but because the walls are interrupted by open arches instead of by windows, this loggia is the very embodiment of inside–outside living.

right through the house, even into the bedrooms. The Dutch eighteenth-century tile panels are used like, and look like, Portuguese *azuelos*.

The soft coral of the dining chairs, which are of classically French appearance with their cabriole legs, and the mushroom-pink of the upholstery to the Chesterfield and armchairs, both traditional and modern, offset each other. The clean lines of the console table pick up the sand colour of the walls, as the mushroom-pink of the armchairs and sofa reflect the colour of the terrazzo. The carved white twiggy pendant candelabra against an interior type white ceiling are vestiges of the internal drawing room.

The bedroom has been given a traditional treatment, lifted by the candy-striped armchair, set amid masses of apricot and cream.

Above left: Life is lived on various levels in the tropics, for the higher you are, the more you catch a cooling breeze. These steps lead to the upper level of the house.

Above right: The side of this lovely house abuts the sea, the view of which is framed by lush, tropical vegetation.

Left: The Venetian window and semicircular fanlight frame perfectly the view of the sea.

Upstairs the master bedroom repeats the French feel of the furniture downstairs in the use of painted furniture, deep-buttoned slipper chair and hangings to a bed-head of French sculptured proportions. The stone cornice and the colours of the fabrics repeat the same themes found downstairs. In the study off this bedroom, the classical theme is repeated in the use of a Venetian window whose view is framed by overhanging trees and palms.

Upper terraces and balconies and lower loggias are floored in the same terrazzo, and an outdoor staircase connects all levels to the swimming pool below. The garden is green with well-irrigated lawns, rich with exotic flowers – hibiscus and tuberose and orchids – and shady with palms and weeping fig, the shiny oval leaves of avocado trees and the long, flat foliage of banana trees. The perfumed admixture of leaf, flower and lime happens simultaneously and, needless to say, the garden is abundant with their fruits.

Certainly this house is lifted by its proximity to

the sea. Unlike gardens of houses sited inland, in which the terrace forms the link between house and garden, this is a property enjoying a series of links to the nethermost extremity – the sea. There is the house, then the loggias, then the encircling band of paths, then the garden and, finally, the sea.

A tropical garden is inevitably lush, and a good deal of management – thinning and pruning, uprooting and replanting – is necessary if it is to maintain its structure and balance. When vegetation is allowed to encroach, you lose the lines and the architecture of the garden and in so doing you lose your view of it as well.

The gates to the world beyond can be seen from the house. On either side of stone piers is a fence of plainly wrought iron. The evanescent flowering of the bougainvillaea beside it is dwarfed by the ancient manchineel tree (*Hippomane mancinella*). All together they are pieces in the jigsaw of the stage set, lending a perspective of the universe to the petty concerns and doings of men and women.

CREATING AN INTEGRATED STYLE

There is a popular misconception that planning a garden is to do with making plants grow and that decorating a house is to do with painting walls. These are important aspects of the styling and decoration of houses and gardens, but they are only a part of the overall picture. Think of your house and garden as a stage set, as a backdrop and as props for the action, which in this case is not a play but real life.

in contemporary terms, the garden spaces have to flow on from the domestic ones. As we have seen, this has not always been so, but what we want now out of garden, or rather the house-cum-garden, is very different from the needs of earlier generations.

Not since Roman times has the logic of linking in with out become clear. Ironically, it has a great deal to do with decreasing amounts of urban and suburban space. It also has to do with the technology and materials that make it feasible – for example, we can use glazed doors, sliding windows or just a sheet of glass.

The first rule of a stage set is that it must permit the necessary movements, exits and entrances of the players. The furniture must not be positioned in such a way that people have to dodge around it and each other. Equally, what really makes a house and a garden work is organizing its space in such a way that a logical sequence of spaces is created. This is a logic both of purpose – the way in which the house and the garden are going to be used – and of aesthetics – how it is going to look when it is arranged in this way or that. This is the overall artistic vision. It is the impression we wish to convey, and it is the effect – or style – that we want to create. Thus, the second rule of the stage set is that it should somehow convey something of the themes of the play. Finally, to be totally successful

The case studies we have described illustrate various ways of linking in with out that are appropriate to different situations – town, country, classic, modern and cottage. To make our points we have often used fairly extreme examples. The reader, sitting in a simple terraced house that is not particularly period, nor particularly modern, nor hanging over an exotic land- or seascape, might well wonder 'but how do I do this? How can I apply these principles to my average house and my average garden plot? How can I integrate in with out to create this special flow you write about? And how much is it all going to cost?'

Left: Echoing the white flowers in the garden, the burst of lilies and marguerites, both standard and potted, enliven this simple conservatory, which was made by glassing over the gap between the house wall and the boundary wall. The conservatory has been given character by both the gabled roof and the arches in the side walls.

WALLS AND WINDOWS

When you are setting out to integrate inside and out, begin by taking your cue from the house and its setting. You are not going to surround a half-timbered mock-Tudor house built in suburban Britain in the 1920s with a garden of elaborate geometric knots and parterres, with a fountain and statuary at every turn. It will sit very well with lawns and Jekyll-type borders, running from hot to cool colour spectrums, with a long, stone-paved terrace to effect the transition. Nor are you going to give a terraced Georgian town house a wilderness of cottage garden planting, any more than you would surround an Elizabethan cottage with a Roman peristyle of colonnades and marble busts. The clean lines of a Georgian façade demand clean lines in the garden and a degree of formality, with clipped trees and shrubs, a long vista culminating a focal point, and a terrace, shaded perhaps by a pergola, not rustic of course, but supported by slim, elegant columns that match the rendering of the façade.

This brings us to a general consideration of colour. It is impossible to lay down hard and fast rules for the colours you use inside and outside your house, but there are a few basic properties of colours of which it would be helpful to be aware when you are planning. Certain colours or groups of colour and their combinations have physical and psychological effects on people. This appears to be true regardless of age or cultural influences. For example, the red group has a stimulating and exciting effect on people, whereas blues and greens are calming and soothing. Not only will your blood pressure and pulse rate rise when you are confronted by colours in the red part of the spectrum and decrease with the blue group, but your emotions will follow suit. Research has shown that when prisoners are housed in red-painted cells they become violent far more quickly than if they are in blue-painted cells. This remains true regardless of their individual preferences for the one colour or the other.

Equally, pale colours expand the size of a room, while dark colours tend to make a room draw in. A

A supremely clever way of integrating inside and out. By using square window panes in the same formation as the floor tiles and by picking a sea colour for the floor, the whole of this room – its walls, windows and floor – presents a unity within itself and with its setting.

pot of red flowers in the middle of the garden will appear to be nearer the viewer than a pot of white flowers. This is not an argument for never using

red in a house or garden, but it is an argument for being careful about where and how you use it.

Let us go back to the mock-Tudor house for a moment. Let us say that it has a large, north-facing room, with French doors leading to a terrace, and you would like to use this room as a study/library

189

and greens and the glimpse of a warm red interior will echo the outdoor scheme as much as terrace planting echoes the indoor scheme when seen from the other point of view.

Using one pale colour or shades of the one colour throughout a house will make the house appear both larger and more unified at the same time, but this is not a principle that needs to be taken to extremes. It is certainly a useful guideline for smaller houses and cottages where space is limited and may be broken up by a number of small rooms but it is not an immutable rule. Clearly a cottage with many beams will have sufficient architectural interest of itself for the walls to be a simple white or pale parchment throughout. And unless you have a very big modern house and a robust sense of humour you are unlikely to prefer a Neapolitan ice-cream look, with one room pink, one green, one white and one red and yellow.

The interior well of this very modern house (left) is a modern atrium. It is, in fact, built as a series of galleries, much along the same lines as some Victorian prisons, although its light airiness and tranquillity mitigate the references to penal architecture. The roof is glass. The galleries and balconies are all solid white, geometric horizontals and square verticals. The doors and walls are white. The flooring is grey and white marble. The long, narrow, rectangular pool or canal running along the centre ground with three small fountains makes a visual and acoustic relief from the hard texture of the surrounding construction.

There are three features that lift this interior. First, the circular portholes in the top of every door, including the front doors and interior doors. The shape is repeated in the oriel window above the front doors and echoed in the fanlight above the window in the end room, like a Venetian window – these last are reminiscent of the Palladian style, the former of 1930s style. Second, the discreet use of brass – the rails and doorknobs – is restrained but fetching, setting off a unified all-white interior with a controlled gleam. Third,

The atrium defines the centre of this modern house. The foliage is essential in relieving the uncompromising style, but is kept restricted – otherwise it might be overwhelming.

or as a formal dining room. There are several good reasons for using reds as your colours here. Because the room is north facing it is never going to be a sunny room. If you use yellow, normally thought of as a 'sunny' colour, you run the risk of making it look very acid because it lacks the sunshine to give it warmth. If you use reds, however, you impart a warmth to the room that it previously lacked. Open the doors on to the terrace and continue the theme outwards with large terracotta pots bursting with red geraniums, with plantings of red-hot pokers behind and some deep green evergreens to set it all off. Seen from the outside the black and white strength of the house will be complemented by the play of reds and probably most importantly, is the use of indoor greenery to dress and soften the walls, the square pillars, and what would otherwise be almost wholly vertical and horizontal. Not only does this create an inside–outside feel, but it gives the interior a natural environment, making it liveable. White is the only possible colour for this interior and the planting makes it green and pleasant.

This French interior (right) has used subtle colour combinations. The walls and planked ceiling are shades of ragged creams and browns, of which the quarry tiled floor is only slightly darker. The ground and surround become unobtrusive while attention is concentrated on the old window-fronted cupboards brushed in a subtle blue-green. It is the window fronts to these cupboards, combined with the habit of dressing them with pleated or stretched fabric, that makes them quintessentially French. The carved wooden column is also typical of the south of France. Its rather charming distressed air comes from leaving the odd flecks of paint on it. These treatments – the choice of colours, the rough brushwork – create a harmony of age and character that is wholly in keeping with an old country house. The actual furniture is, in a sense, immaterial. The same cupboards could be used in a Paris apartment, but you would not then expect a quarry tiled floor and rough brushwork. Integration is not only a question of house and garden: it is also about setting, location, age and type of property.

You can carry colour from the inside of the house through the transition areas into the garden. Again, the same applies. Blocks of the same colour will have a bigger impact and greater design strengths than a series of small containers with lots of different colours, whose effect is usually fiddly and messy. This is not to say, of course, that you should not mix colours at all. If, for example, you have used a warm cream for the hall, stairs and landing, you could move to a paler and cooler shade of the same colour for the drawing room, or you could leave it the same, or you could deepen it so that it is on the elegant side of yellow. The

paintwork is white, there are touches of blue and green in the room, or apricot and blue. It is simplicity itself to wed these colours to the planting in the conservatory or on the terrace as a transition to the rest of the garden.

In the conservatory climbing plumbago, with its mass of florets like so many pale blue skies, or enormous pots of deep blue lavender on the terrace, or fragile lace-cap hydrangeas and climbing roses, like 'Golden Showers' or the vigorous shrub rose 'Buff Beauty', which bears on the same plant blooms of palest butter to deep gold, for it changes colour as it ages, can all be set against a vivid green leaf. Or you might mix these colours with the deep apricot of chaenomeles

Cupboards decorated with rough dragging line the walls of the passage, and are complemented by the quarry tile flooring. In keeping with traditional French style, the cupboard doors are lined with fabric.

Dressing a window that overlooks a very green garden with predominantly green fabric is a happy choice, and one that has been emphasized by the green-painted washstand.

(Japanese quince or flowering quince) and clumps of eschscholzia (Californian poppy), with its white, saffron and rust or terracotta flowers and feathery foliage. The effect of working variations of the same colours outside as you use inside will be to create an easy transition between the two.

The way in which you treat the windows should follow the same principles. You do not want to create hard, shut-off blocks between inside and out with lengths of fabric whose colours or patterns are at odds with what lies behind them. You could ruin all the good work you have done in blending inside colour with out in the above scheme at a stroke by introducing grey louvered blinds or burnt orange dralon curtains. Although it would be wonderful, you do not have to go the expense of silk curtains, dyed the same colour as the walls, because there are all sorts of inexpensive ways in which you can make a room elegant. If you are using paint, try small tins of two or three possible shades on separate pieces of board. You can then not only prop them up in various parts of the room to see how the colour will be affected by different lights – near the window, in a dark corner and so forth – but you can also take them with you when choosing fabrics. There are lots of alternatives to expensive fabrics – cotton sheeting, lining fabric, unbleached calico or muslin, can, provided they are used in sufficient quantity and are cleverly draped, look every bit as good if not better than vastly more expensive materials.

A word or two about the minimalist look, and this also applies if you are fortunate enough to live in an old house with shutters. Windows without any form of curtaining at all or with only a simple white straight blind or with shutters alone may have enormous dramatic impact by day, but you must consider their effect at night. There is nothing more chilling to the heart than a black November night framed all evening in your windows unless it is the stark white of a pulled-down blind of the kind more usually found in the clinical surroundings of a sanatorium. Shutters in old houses can be equally stark and unwelcoming. Not only does fabric soften and, in comparison to these alternatives, warm a room, it also helps to soak up sound. You will find that, especially in a room with hard flooring, the clatter and echoes are greatly diminished when you hang curtains.

The exception to this rule is the sort of treatment

given to the doors (above). The blue shutters are the outer doors to the hall. When they are open you can look through the inner glass doors straight through the hall, through the same repeated arrangement of doors to the other side of the garden beyond. Like the town houses of ancient Rome, in which as soon as you were through the front door you could see the garden behind, so with this conversion of an old agricultural building you can look straight through the house, as it were, enjoying a different landscape on either side. In a building like this, of course, you need no form of curtaining: the inner glass doors are almost invisible and the steel blue outer shutters both act as security doors and at the same time frame the entrance. This particular blue is a good choice too. It provides a strong contrast with the red of the brickwork, it does not look drab, as green might look, and it does not look as pointless as white might do, nor as garish as yellow would. All in all, it is a highly effective solution.

Right: The blue shutters on this door open outwards, while a secondary glass door opens inwards. The detail is repeated at the other side of an entrance hall, so that you see the countryside beyond, right through the house.

FLOORINGS

This is the hardest used of all surfaces, and it is also, of course, the ground on which everything else – walls and furniture and doors – rests. Bear in mind that at the points of integration with the outside – the front door, French or sliding windows, a balcony door and so on – it is going to be hardest used of all. Immediately, therefore, we have the twin problems of looks and – or, more often, versus – practicality.

The important thing about creating a flow from inside to out is that the one should appear to meld into the other with a degree of appropriateness that makes the transition not necessarily imperceptible, but at least comfortable. What one seeks to avoid is a sense of disjuncture, whereby the interior feels at odds with its surroundings. This principle requires very subtle interpretation, and it does not require to be taken to extremes or to the bitter end of its logical conclusion. We are not suggesting that if you live in a modern house with lots of glass, surrounded by grass and deciduous trees, the way to integrate inside and out would be to carpet the entire house with artificial turf, to hang green curtains in the spring and summer, yellow and red curtains in the autumn and no curtains at all in the winter.

What we are saying is that a wall-to-wall velvet pile carpet of royal blue with woven scrolls of gold, of the type normally found in smart London hotels or theatre foyers, would be wrong. What would be appropriate would be, say, sanded and varnished floorboards of blond wood, or pale woodblock with rugs for the sitting and dining areas – new ethnic or old Turkey or even fine faded Persian or Aubusson. The rugs provide warmth, colour and comfort, and the wood is the most natural material you could use to echo the outside. Sisal carpeting is another 'natural' material, as is sea-grass, but even the finest of these is a very hard, knobbly form of floor covering. Stylistically there is nothing to prevent you from laying wall-to-wall carpet, and everything to recommend it if the floor is concrete: the trick is to keep it plain and understated, a colour that does

The simplicity of natural materials, such as this timber flooring, emphasizes the tranquil continuity from outside to in. Without any furniture, this room would have a Japanese feel.

not draw attention to itself and thereby distract from the view through the windows or the clean lines of the architecture and furniture.

This modern house (above) has, effectively, got glazed walls – they are sliding doors that give straight on to the garden. But it is not a garden of blue and pink and yellow flowers – it is a tranquil

garden of shrubs, grass, trees and stones. The overall picture is green, although in autumn the Japanese maples glow deep red and the tangle of shrubbery goes bare-stemmed into winter. There is something very solid and right about the pine strip flooring to the room inside. Partly, of course, it is because it is a natural material, taken up by the

living forms in the garden. It blends harmoniously – or perhaps we are predisposed to see this – with the other materials of nature such as grass and stones. Also, because it is only semi-separated from the outside by glass and because you can see the outside at the same time, the pine strip makes an appropriate flooring for the interior.

Grey tiles are a good contrast with the wet black tiles and with the metal chairs on this terrace in Sydney. The gradual demarcation between the awning and the terrace permits a smooth transition from house to garden.

feel to the room and make it appear immeasurably smaller. Generally speaking, of course, a dark ground and/or walls tend to draw a room in, while light colours expand a room outwards. There could be an argument for using a cold, dark ground, but the architecture would need to be ultra-modern, and the room would have to very large and also very light. Against a backdrop of white walls, white fittings and white furniture, the effect would be dramatic.

With a modern backdrop, such as the pink-stained walls seen here, a grey ceramic tiled floor and steps on different levels sit against the pink retaining walls and create a glossy black ground for the water spout. The symmetry of chairs and tables, the confluence of black, pink and grey is all rendered more approachable by the impermanence of the chequered cloth awning, which is both light and simple. What makes this composition of a piece – and we shall see this message repeated time and again – is the planting behind. A mass of foliage of various hues and textures often compensates for a deficiency in the use of man-made materials.

Although the mix of pink and grey, now used throughout the interiors of building societies and hairdressers and show-houses is, by and large, unpleasant, the subtler mix of such shades can be effective. The black ground under the spout (left) pulls the scene together. The only problems are the textures of the surfaces, which can be slippery in winter.

If none of these conditions pertain, and the house is only moderately modern, the room is not of immense proportions and so on, but you do want the inside to echo something of the outside, you could use light ceramic tiles for the majority of the flooring and make a border of dark tiles. Alternatively you could use dark diamond inserts between the lighter tiles all the way through the room or use a chequerboard effect, alternating dark and light.

In older houses the link to the outside is often through the kitchen-dining room, and this is

If your house is very modern and situated in an urban environment, perhaps with a small garden, largely paved, and with a large sliding glass door from the living room to the outside, you could use any of the above treatments, but you could also use ceramic tiles, especially if they were the same colour as the paving. But what if the paving consists of those very dark blue or dark red, smooth engineering bricks? Ceramic tiling of the same colour or even continuing the brick indoors would not only be very expensive but would make the interior very dark. It would also impart a cold particularly true of town houses where the semi-basement has been converted to provide one big kitchen/eating/family area with a sliding door or French windows at the back and steps up to the garden. It is also often true of cottages, where a couple of small rooms have been knocked together to make a kitchen-dining room. The flooring in both these areas is going to take a lot of hard use, and quarry tiles of one sort or another are a logical and practical treatment.

But beware. There is nothing so odd in a town house surrounded by a lot of other town houses as a rustic farmhouse kitchen with exposed beams over the hob, oak doors and drawer fronts, and large, chunky, rather coarse floor tiles whose influences owe more to Spain or South America than they do to an English farmhouse and are even further removed from the urban environment. Restraint becomes all important. If the outside of your cottage has a path of old herringbone brick of faded red, do not use ochre-based quarry tiles in the kitchen-dining room that leads on to it. If the exterior of the basement of the town house uses yellowish bricks for its supporting wall and floor, use a softer version of the colour for the inside.

This modern house (right) uses large red, square-laid quarry tiles, the only furniture being a big double circular oak dining table and traditional capstan oak chairs. Nevertheless, it is a very modern rendering of age-old themes. One entire wall is taken up with sliding glass doors, but you notice how the floor tiles are continued for a good two courses beyond the doors. The fact that once out of the protection of the overhang and walls, the flooring changes to slab paving matters not a jot. The point is that it has been continued beyond the confines of the interior and thus gone to meet the exterior half-way.

This gives the inside and the outside something in common. How else has this communality been expressed? Well, for one thing the beams are reddened to reflect the flooring; for another, there are plants and foliage in abundance inside the house – more, in fact, than there is on the terrace

outside. This has the effect of creating an interior garden, which prepares the visitor for the garden outside. If you are going to use very deep colours – such as this dark cherry red for the floor tiles – you must reflect its depth in some way somewhere else. The deep dark green foliage performs this function, and if you imagine this room without it, the effect would be bare and stark rather than warm and rich.

Suppose you have an old country house with a worn stone-flagged kitchen or a stone-flagged hall, all dips and unevenness, or a farmhouse, say, with

The warmth of the polished red quarry tiles used inside is carried outside, beyond the sliding doors, to the first step of this Californian house.

Left: The gleaming white, enhanced by white and grey marble tiling, unifies this dining room with the atrium beyond. The rug beneath the dining table signals that this is an interior room.

Right: Pale honey quarry tiles are suitable flooring for a country hall where the walls are rough rendered and stone. Notice how this floor area is subtly differentiated from the passage beyond by a slight change in the colour and the pattern in which the tiles are laid.

a slate floor in the kitchen and hall. You are not going to rip it up. If it is in the hall, you can lay a good strong rug or two in the area nearest the rest of the doors – nearest the front door the surface will look after itself and the muddy boots, too. If you are lucky you will have old stone or slate outside the house as well. If not, take your cue from the house and use stone or slate for the terrace. If you can track down older worn stone so much the better. There is absolutely no point in turning a traditional building that has grown out of

the history and geography of its surroundings into a hacienda or a Dallas ranch.

The guiding principle is to have respect for architectural integrity, not just of fine and important houses, but of vernacular buildings as well. We have seen three-hundred-year-old cottages with all their character, funny little draughty bedroom fireplaces, long passages, uneven floors, knocked out of them to make Spanish arches and ethnic tiled walls and floors. You can make a house comfortable and modernize it, but only up to a certain point. Do not throw out good taste with the rotten architrave.

FURNISHINGS

In this wedding-breakfast-look, the romance of loosely gathered white fabric is undeniably effective – no other colour would yield the same effect. The trellis-backed chairs keep the effect light and airy, but the simplicity of the arrangement would be equally in keeping with period or modern houses.

We have seen throughout how feasible it is in most houses to mix antique with modern, and how one genuine piece, albeit shabby and dilapidated, is worth its weight in a hundred reproduction pieces. But it goes without saying that if you have a very definite look to the interior of your house – heavy carved medieval furniture, all chests and linenfold panelling, or light and delicate Louis XV gilded armchairs and Aubusson carpets, or minimalist modern furniture – you will not want to use moulded white plastic on the terrace.

What we want to talk about here is choosing appropriate furniture, tableware and ornaments for transitional areas such as the conservatory and the terrace. The emphasis is again on using material appropriate to both the setting and the interior. If the interior is dark and medieval you could use dark-stained timber chairs with a tall, high back. Iroko, a hardwood frequently used for outdoor furniture, can be happily left outside. It weathers to a silvery grey or it can be re-stained. Some modern iron furniture, with very plain lines, is equally suitable. Alternatively, if inside is light and delicate, fine trellised furniture with a hint of chinoiserie to it will look more in keeping than endless curlicues of wrought iron. Minimalist modern interiors might equally well use the same iron as medievalists but may just as likely use any number of good plain natural materials as those thrown up by modern technologies.

The simplicity, elegance and grace of this modern terrace is timeless. The look – both modern and classical – is achieved by restricting the colour to white, which immediately unifies everything, by using the simplest of patterns – in this case trellis for the chairs (trellising is one of the oldest patterns in the world) and by using a great deal of simply pleated and looped fabric for the curtains. Part of the charm of the curtains is that they lend an interior feel to an essentially exterior place. There are, in fact, no windows. The overall impression is much the same as that created in Moorish or Turkish courtyards, or the outdoor dining rooms of ancient Rome, or the palace courtyard mentioned in the Book of Esther. Such courtyards were open, used for dining and entertaining, but they were also furnished.

In a climate that guarantees months of continuous sunshine there is no reason why courtyards and cloisters should not be furnished. In less temperate areas, where it could rain at any time, it would not be practical unless there was a way of quickly and simply putting up and taking down such hangings or perhaps swooping them back under cover. If such a terrace were large enough, it would make a most delightful place for a summer wedding breakfast, for this way of dressing a terrace has all the charm of a marquee and none of its temporary qualities.

If you have a stone-flagged sitting area bounded by a drystone wall, or a small area of herring-bone brick outside your eighteenth-century cottage, resin recliners from Sweden are going to look somewhat out of keeping. In any case, they will probably take up far too much space and dwarf an already small area. This is not to say that this sort of furniture is inherently bad. It is not. Some of it is very stylish, and it is certainly very comfortable. There is many a dark green resin recliner with simple striped cushions (not the floral variety) that looks very good indeed. But it might be better, from the point of view of space and looks in this particular case, to take it down to the bottom of the garden, further away from the constrictions imposed by the architecture of the house, and place it under the apple tree. A wooden slatted reclining chair like the old chairs that are used on the decks of liners, is more in keeping if you have the space.

Similarly, in a Victorian-style conservatory, a simple built-in window seat and a couple of old Lloyd Loom armchairs is going to work much better than over-elaborate wrought ironwork or a suite of patterned Taiwanese basketwork. Do not be afraid to put things together. The iron supports from old treadle sewing machines make a good base for a table. Use one either end for a long rectangular table, like a trestle table, and finish it

In a room such as this – the entrance to Beatrix Potter's farmhouse – a traditional oak drop-leaf table and chairs are the most appropriate furniture, especially when they are dominated by a well-blacked range.

both its integrity and its self-respect. Second, and because of the first characteristic, it is as integrated as it has ever needed to be with its exterior. The stone-flagged floor is practical and serviceable for muddy shoes and boots – the Lake District is not noted for endless hours of continuous sunshine. There are rugs for comfort where you sit, whether it is at the fire or the table. The polished furniture and brass, and the china treasures speak of industry and self-respect. From an interior like this, you would expect outside drystone walls in good repair and neat rows of cabbages and lettuces, well-hoed in between – and you would get it. Houses such as this were made to be warm and homely refuges from the hard work that hill farming demands. It would be as ludicrous to tack a 'Victorian-style' conservatory on to this room as it would to stuff it with Corinthian columns and rococo pier glasses.

On the other hand, a smart modern house or villa is not going to make an appropriate setting for rustic, rough-hewn garden furniture. Something that looks like a collection of branches ripped off the nearest tree may be entirely suitable for a simple country dwelling but it's going to lose a great deal of charm in a glamorous context. If on the other hand you have a nice old stone cottage or converted farm building or farmhouse in France or Italy which looks suitably decayed and ancient, if not exactly tumble-down, the rustic look can be quite charming. Try to keep it simple though and use traditional and local style. A simple trestle table of planks of wood jollified with local pottery will be more effective than anything.

The American designer Keeyla Meadows has a small garden only 13.7 metres (45 feet) square in the middle of San Francisco. The plot is surrounded by other buildings but not so that you'd notice because what she has done has been to turn it into a cottage garden jumble filled with trees, including apple, crab apple and weeping cherry, climbers, such as wisteria, roses and clematis, and the old favourites of delphinium, lavender and forget-me-nots. Surrounded by so many soft colours, which flow

off with a marble or marbleized top or a top that is painted to look like stone.

In a traditional cottage there may be little or no scope for terraces or conservatories. There may be nothing more than a garden path and a front door, with a back door out to the vegetable garden. In this case, the hall, or the parlour, or whatever is the first room you walk into assumes greater importance because it becomes the only transitional area to use for scene-setting. The photograph (above) shows the entrance hall to Beatrix Potter's small farmhouse at Sawrey in the Lake District. The stone-flagged floor is warmed by a small carpet and a rag rug in front of the range. Well-polished horse brasses and a copper warming pan hang over the fireplace and the dark painted panelling and woodwork is typical of this sort of house. The floral paper on the ceiling is also typical and helped to disguise many a crack or uneven surface.

There are two important characteristics of this room. First, it is wholly unpretentious. It has been kept in the way such houses were furnished and decorated in that part of England at that time. There has been no stripping of paint, no smartening up with fake beams, and no intrusion with Peruvian rugs or ceiling spotlights. It retains

Maroon, purple and green are used for everything, from blinds to bedspread, from light fittings to paintwork, in Keeyla Meadows' bedroom. The surprising colour choice works well, primarily because it has been used so consistently.

The restrained but elegantly dressed curtains (notice the subtle use of the check lining) allows attention to be focused on the club fender around the late Victorian fireplace. It is important to leave the things you want to emphasize to speak for themselves.

into each other, together with the plain and simple architecture of the house, the urban setting is out of sight and out of mind.

As a sculptor turned garden designer, Keeyla Meadows works with every form of the plastic arts. As the look of the garden is predominantly rural, she has been able to reflect this in her furnishings.

Simple country chairs surround the dining table laid with her own pottery plates and dishes in pinks, blues and yellows, which look both rustic and modern at the same time. Hand-made ceramics are often ideal tableware in simple cottages in sunny climates. The same quality carries through to the garden furniture. She has designed her benches, painted in blue-grey and mauve-pink, to give the same feel of rustic modern, their colours and shapes making them highly individual and artistic as well as reflecting the silver-greys and pinks of her plants. The carry-through from the planting to the benches to the tableware makes this an essay in integration on every level.

But suppose you have spent all your money on buying a smart period townhouse and you have only the time and money to go and buy a plastic table. There is nothing inherently sinful about a plastic table – it depends what you do with it. One innocent thing to do, which hardly counts as pretentious, is to cover it with a plain white cloth for your outdoor lunch or dinner party, and if you have run out of large white tablecloths a large white sheet will do just as well.

THE JUNCTION

Right: A screened metal decking links the first floor of an older house around a new ground-floor extension and thus to the garden beyond, incidentally providing a sort of pergola to the opening windows below.

Opposite above: A recess has been beamed over in this Spanish garden and covered with split bamboo to create shade. Furnished with smart cane furniture and a few plants, the area becomes a new garden room.

Opposite below: This continental porch has had curtains added to smarten up an outside eating place. Lavender, rosemary and two forms of jasmine must make the area heady with their fragrance.

For maximum effect the integration of in with out is achieved at the planning stage so that the form of building itself creates the link. A recent contemporary addition by architect Jeremy Cockayne to an older house connects its first floor with a rear garden by a screened metal decking system and stairs, the deck incidentally providing a pergola surround to the small terrace below (above). Sliding doors link a dining room with the paved terrace, which is furnished with planted pots. The

terrace is paved with concrete slabs separated by a sealed timber fillet. A strip of gravel at the edge of the terrace allows for a drainage run off.

In warmer climates odd corners of a terrace can be exploited to create an outside room. The pergola structure (left), bridging a recess in the garden, is covered with split bamboo to create its room effect. A carpet of terracotta tiles infills the stone of the terrace, and basket furniture has been introduced to create a shaded leisure area. In winter the split bamboo can be rolled back to allow the sun to warm up such an inviting corner. The building is, in fact, a plant room and changing space for the swimming pool beyond, making the space doubly useful.

Colour washing walls tends to be a technique reserved for warmer climates, too, but used in a subtle way, colour can also integrate odd spaces such as this so that it reads as part of an entity.

With decreasing garden space we seek to have physical if not visual access to every corner of our limited domestic gardens where previously those who had pleasure gardens needed only to make inroads into its wildness, or actually seek a sanctuary from it. Between these extremes different ages have altered and adapted according to fashion to create different garden styles. It is all to do with how we regard nature, where we are located and the sort of house in which we live.

Very much in the current idiom – for it could be located anywhere – is this terrace setting (left). The porch linking into it could be built in a dozen different ways. The furniture is mixed and casual, but it is not too smart that it does not look lived in. The surfacing of the terrace is of random stone with grass between the slabs which a hover mower would keep in order. Low-growing thymes could provide an alternative, fragrant planting if it did not receive too much hard wear. The spectacular central climber is *Trachelospermum jasminoides*, a very fragrant evergreen, with normal jasmine on the right. In the foreground grows the upright form of *Rosmarinus officinalis* (rosemary), with lavender beyond.

Opposite: In a traditional English cottage the door opens outwards onto a limestone paved terrace. This arrangement was sometimes necessary when a door that opened inwards might have impeded an internal passage.

Only latterly, with a decreasing amount of available, often suburban space, has the logic of linking in with out become clear. At its simplest it is essential that access links home and garden. The traditional country door, for instance, may open outwards, linking the interior, which is almost at the same level as the paved terrace outside. Seating is provided by an unsophisticated stone bench with cushions. It could not be simpler.

Where access is not possible, planting against the house can help, and on older buildings one often sees an evergreen *Magnolia grandiflora* providing this connection. Larger windows give an illusion from inside of a connection with out, and a suitable garden design relating to their size will help – a pool the window's width, for instance – but for a physical spatial flow, windows to the floor should open in the manner of French doors, sliding doors and so on.

Huge sliding doors in this American home link to a timber deck, which surrounds an old oak tree, growing at a lower level. From the deck timber, steps lead to a lower part of the garden.

We saw that some of the early modern buildings of this century, mainly in the United States, used enormous areas of glass – Philip Johnson's own house, Mies van der Rohe's Farnsworth House, the Neutra House, Arizona, and so on – so that you were virtually living among the trees in the landscape or above the desert. As spectacular as these structures are, for those living in colder climates the combination of heating and double glazing in winter, along with shading and air conditioning in summer, make this degree of glazing an expensive option.

The configuration of the building often helps to create an integration as we have seen. An area of the house may partially enclose some of the site, for example, even if it is only a garage wall. Increasingly, conservatories are being added to the rear of a house (they are another subject in themselves), but they do have the effect of creating an area out from the house and providing a sheltered and, therefore, usable corner, too.

It would be ideal if the level could carry through opening doors, but where this is not possible a step is sometimes necessary down to the garden. The step should be fairly wide – too narrow a step can be dangerous. The windows of the American house illustrated (left) sweep back to link to a timber deck, which surrounds a gnarled oak tree growing up from a much lower level. Timber steps from the deck link it to the remainder of the garden at an intermediate height.

If you then add a pergola over your doorway, or along a blank façade of an adjacent wall, when the pergola is covered with greenery, you begin to create not only shade in summer, but a sort of half-way house. It provides something to be under while being open at the sides. For those on the ground floor of apartment blocks, or living cheek by jowl in town, a pergola can provide privacy from above as well. Pergola structures are very varied, their design having to do with both the building they adjoin in one context or the mood you are seeking to create in a wider one of the whole garden.

PERGOLAS

Right: This directional pergola, forming a viewpoint from the house, is constructed of wooden arches and is hung most beautifully with roses.

The pergola structure, like the concept of the cloister, provides access, often around a central courtyard. Used for covering access in the garden, the pergola may be linear, providing shade on a path and leading from one place to another. This type of traditional pergola may create a tunnel of flowers to stroll under in a leisurely fashion. The structure can be arched or square, according to the desired effect.

Pergolas provide the ideal opportunity for vertical planting. Heavily clothed with climbers – roses, wisteria and vines – they embody all the romanticism of an English country garden. But another sort of pergola to delineate and cover a space for eating out or sitting will be less linear and far wider. Both the frequency and the thickness of the horizontals you use and the planting you introduce will affect the mood of the structure you have created.

Above: A South African pergola which provides a shaded outside room and supports a grape vine. The structure was built with the house, not added as an afterthought. Floor tiles and colour wash are the same.

Where you are fixing pergola horizontals to a house the frequency you use them will depend on the rhythm of the window, wall and door relationship. Their height and dimensions will to some degree be determined by the style of the building. A brick-built, single-storey house in South Africa (above) has a wide pergola that covers an outside dining room. The piers of the pergola are also in brick, painted to match the

house. Stained timber horizontals fit between the roof eaves and the top of the window adjoining this space. A vine grows over the pergola, which, when out of leaf in winter, allows light into the house but which, when in leaf in summer, provides very necessary shade. An added bonus are the grapes in autumn, which can be picked for the table. The flooring is of terracotta concrete.

Most pergola horizontals are of timber, but strained wire, metal and even a synthetic material

width of a pergola, its material and its frequency with the verticals to hold it up, which can of course be fewer since you may use a cross brace. As in most building detail, the more simple your solution the better the final result will look. Incidentally, it is not necessary to disturb the fabric of a structure to hang a horizontal on it. Simple metal shoes are available, and these can be plugged to the wall so that the horizontal can sit in them.

Often brick or stone piers are too massive for the horizontals that they support. Always make sure that the timbers you use are in proportion with the piers. If you are contemplating a pergola, draw up some alternatives to scale before you make any decisions and see what works best with the fabric of your house. Remember that climbing plants growing over a pergola can be quite heavy, and bear in mind that a plant's bulk added to your structure will visually enlarge it enormously. It is also important to make sure that your planting is deciduous on the structure so that you do not obstruct light in winter. A vine, of course, is ideal.

At the turn of the century the loggia or porch was constructed over a service door, quite open, making a useful place to take off and store muddy boots and to leave the secateurs and so on. An extension of the loggia idea, although more to create shade, was the veranda or stoop, which surrounded many colonial homes. Such a space was very much an outside room, good for breakfast or sundowners.

Many of these types of structure can be adapted to individual situations, although as soon as the structure is envisaged, consider whether planning permission is necessary.

Above: Shades of Giverny – this metal hooped pergola is hung with ripening marrows. The path beneath is edged with nasturtiums and rudbeckia.

Left: A Mediterranean pergola, with softwood horizontals sitting on squared stone piers. A beautiful white wisteria clothes the structure.

would be entirely suitable in some situations. Rather more crucial and more difficult to detail, is the vertical to hold the structure up – its dimensions, frequency and material. There seems to be a visually balanced relationship between the

TERRACES

In the Riviera sunshine this stone terrace is not pinched in proportions. There is ample space to relax and entertain. Conversely, its intimate, shaded arrangement would give pleasure to the solitary sunbather as well.

Hard surfacing is one of the major design elements of a garden and one of its many forms can be used to provide a link between in and out. The same material could be used for the flat planes of interior and exterior surfacing, and their correct proportionate relationship is important, for there is a satisfaction in seeing across a room to a correctly proportioned terrace beyond. This works on any scale. And in reverse a terrace needs to be wide enough to provide a satisfactory base to a house.

and totally visually undemanding. Adjacent to the house, a further room-like shade is provided by enormous, plain linen umbrellas sunk directly into the terrace. Dark coloured, though plain, cushion covers complement the umbrellas. Huge terracotta pots of white oleander soften and cool the terrace, which is a set designed for people. Sun-bronzed, dressed minimally in brilliant Côte d'Azure blue, yellow and orange, this is an exquisite understated setting, whose proportions are both comfortable for a few but ample for many.

It is the proportions of a house that give a clue to the proportions of, first, a terrace and then subsequent garden elements leading from it. Very broadly, the dimension of floor to ceiling expressed usually by window height, when translated to terrace width, gives a satisfactory basic dimension. It will be in the region of 2.5 to 3 metres (8 to 10 feet). This dimension can be increased by proportionate increments to include the rest of a layout. Changes of level can be accommodated into the basic module along with linking steps or ramps.

The material used for the terrace will depend on the style and period of building and, of course, available finance. The more complicated a ground pattern and the smaller the elements used to construct it, the more expensive it will be, since labour costs will be higher.

Brick and stone are the preferred surfacings, and both brick for paving and stone slabs are now simulated in concrete as well. The slabs are excellent, but for the domestic market clay bricks are still preferred. Clay pavoirs, which look like bricks, are a preferred option to building brick because they are slightly larger and thinner. A building brick has to be used on its side in a paving pattern to reduce the area of frost action on it, and the outer edges are the hardest, having the higher firing in the kiln. So a pavoir is much more economical. Those machine finished with a wire cut have a good foot-holding texture to them, because some bricks, particularly very hardy, dark

Brick piers set in a circular pattern provide the hard surface to this entrance court.

The warmer the climate, of course, the more the terrace will be used, and sun loungers require a lot of space. The surface of the amply proportioned terrace illustrated (above) in the south of France is of squared stone, which is textured for bare feet

West Country limestones are available in a variety of sizes and thicknesses. A delivery is made by weight, and stones are usually assorted, which means that any design with them has to considered on site.

Both brick and stone may be used internally as well as externally. Before commissioning a builder to lay brick or stone for you, try to see some of their work. Stone should not need to have angles cut out of it, and courses between the slabs or brick should be mortared and slightly rubbed back. Butt jointing – that is, slabs or bricks pushed together with no mortar between, only sand – is probably not sound enough for a terrace area adjacent to the house. This sort of terrace should also be laid on a concrete base for stability. Always consider falls away from the structure when laying any sort of paving, and consider a drainage plan – that is, where surplus water will go in a heavy downpour. Normal rain is not a problem, it is the occasional downpour that can flood, because water needs to be led away quickly to a soakaway.

Slate can provide an excellent flooring for a garden room or a conservatory and the surface can be carried outside as well. Since slate is expensive, if it is not quarried near where you live, it could be combined with another material outdoors to lessen its expense. The great virtue of slate is that it can be supplied in an extremely thin tile form and can therefore be laid on a bed correcting unevennesses in say an old property, be laid on to of another surface or be used to floor a balcony or terrace with a minimum of weight.

There are plenty of other hard tiles available, which are suitable for inside use, but Italian or French terracotta sadly is not frostproof when used outdoors. Wood is used in Britain, on the Continent and in North America as a decking material and is excellent, but it does not really lend itself to indoor use, because with humidity it becomes slippery and subsequently rots.

Some of the patterning pressed into coloured and textured concrete is impressive, and there is a sealed aggregate finish that would be ideal for both an inside and outside use. By far the greatest number

Another stone terrace. The colour blends well with the Portuguese villa. Doors open out, providing easy access for serving the table. The use of dark green for woodwork and upholstery complements the house colour and the hanging lemons.

engineering bricks, can become very slippery when wet and, therefore, dangerous.

There are a multitude of bricks available on the market, and it is wise to match up to any brick already used in the structure of your house. London stock bricks, which were used for much of the construction of the Victorian development there, and the surrounding property walls, are used second-hand, because new stock bricks are bright yellow. When contemplating using building brick on edge within a project, investigate the use of old bricks as well as new.

Squared or rectangular stone paving is invariably not new, and fresh cut and dressed stone is prohibitively expensive. Old Yorkstone and various of people probably use pre-cast concrete slabs as their terrace finish and the range of texture is now excellent if you shop around. A textured finish is safest for outside use – and the same slab can be used inside but turned over where the surface is flat and then sealed. It looks very good with rugs or mats on top of it. Not all concrete slabs lend themselves however to this treatment.

Possibly the most satisfactory hard surface treatment is a mixture of materials. All the same, brick on walls and floor can look too hard, and too wide an area of slab, whether stone or concrete, can look drab. Break up your pattern with either a geometric design, although not too much of one, or lay a random combination – smaller brick rivulet infills through large slabs, for instance, or a carpet of tiles surrounded by a border of slab.

There is an extraordinary terrace in California that incorporates blue tiles into a mixture of brick and random stone. It is curiously attractive, especially used with yellow ranunculus and blue delphiniums.

The coping along the vertical timber retaining walls to the site are also capped with blue tile.

In general, random paving, which we in Britain call crazy-paving, is rarely successful. Carefully cut larger slabs at set at random angles are acceptable, but the hotchpotch effect of the kind that the jobbing gardener lays as his speciality, too often only perpetuates its name.

Holidays have undoubtedly influenced the manner in which we think of the terrace. It is a place for lazy meals under hot sun. The conservatory, as we have seen, extends this dream for those who live in less sunny areas, but the subtler use of warm colour can relieve winter greyness. Earth colours of chrome, ochre and burnt sienna evoke north Italy and terracotta – red earth – gives a feeling of warmth.

Terracotta tiles floor this terrace working well with the corn yellow of the house. An unusual touch is the use of midnight blue for paintwork and upholstery. The lemons are a masterly final touch.

Glazed tiles are combined with random stone and brick in this San Francisco garden. The wall coping is also glazed, for there is, of course, no frost hazard.

CONSERVATORIES AND GARDEN ROOMS

There is an increasing vogue for conservatories.
Drive through almost any new development and
you will see these 'modules' stuck on to the backs
of the houses, as if they are necessary sales
gimmicks. But these 'crystal rooms', as Clough
Williams Ellis, a twentieth-century British
architect, called them, have quite a tradition,
progressing from eighteenth-century orangeries,
through often huge Victorian structures to our
present-day mini-form.

There are also traditional forms of commercial
lean-to, follies and glass loggias, which have all
been adapted to provide this covered green oasis.
For that is what they can be. Many people simply
use them as an extension to the home, as a place
for summer eating – winter, too, if well heated –
but unless they are large enough it is difficult to
combine both living and any degree of planting,
for our requirements are different from those of
the plants. Your success will depend on the type of
plants you want to grow, because the permutations
of temperature, humidity and aspect are endless.

First of all, as a living space, the conservatory is
wonderful throughout autumn, winter and early
spring, and even on cool summer evenings as the
dew comes down. They are very much the sort of
place in which to relax, read the Sunday papers
and snooze. But even in winter or on a sunny day
both adequate ventilation and, more importantly,
shade are necessary whenever the sun shines. The
smaller the conservatory, the more quickly it will
heat up, and then cool down when ventilated. So
where you have the option, choose as large as a
structure as possible.

In southwest London the architect Pierre
d'Avoine has created a wonderful structure fitting
logically on to a standard, large-gabled, brick
Edwardian house (right). The addition works
rather like a veranda, except that it is at garden
level rather than set high. The large glass full-
height windows slide open so that the garden can
be enjoyed through the filtered light from a huge
old wisteria that was preserved throughout the
building operations. The climber was originally

A garden room that
extends across the
front of an old
house and
incorporates an
extension, too,
thereby giving an
ordinary, rather
boxy, London semi-
detached house a
new lease of life.

over a structure linking to the older part of the house. Such a room, while being definitely a useful addition to the home (it is down two steps from the kitchen and dining area), also allows the feel of the garden to flow right in to the house – with the doors open wide its birdsong and scents in summer permeate the whole living space.

A more conventional conservatory structure imposes itself in to the garden, by opening its double doors so that one's guests are virtually sitting in the garden itself. The floor is black and white tiled and upon it palms are grouped in terracotta pots to create a feel of exoticism. Without shading, these structures can become exceedingly hot, so cane shading has been tailored to the window dimensions of this roof and can be pulled up and lowered like blinds.

Into your conservatory or garden room you can introduce pots of early bulbs, or perhaps a small tree in a pot – some form of citrus, perhaps, which can be put outside in summer. Too much vegetation is difficult to maintain, for plants do not like the dry atmosphere in which we live, and with that comes insect infestation, which is difficult to spray or eradicate over carpet or upholstery.

The plantsperson can find that a conservatory is a paradise, for divided only by a pane of glass on a dull January day, you may ignore the sleet and rain outside and inside transport yourself to the Mediterranean with flowers and fragrances from plants that grow, ideally, both in the ground and in containers. Trees, shrubs and climbers with a huge range of bulbs can give you pleasure right through the winter, the range of plants you select determined by your heating capacity. Even a conservatory with no heating at all and only protected from the wind allows for a really early

spring indoors. A small area of water encourages some humidity in the atmosphere, which the plants prefer – the more tropical the mood, the greater the degree of humidity is necessary. Pave the area with tile or slab, and into your green mass you may introduce the odd chair and a table.

Go for a Mediterranean mood with plumbago, bougainvillea, agapanthus, citrus, cassia, mimosa, mandervilla, passion flowers and so on. The more exotic you become, the more growth the plants put on and the more cutting back will be necessary. A Mediterranean selection of plants needs no extra heat in summer, just plenty of sun and air, but your selection will need some slight heat in winter. Humidity is not a priority. A sub-tropical mood will need humidity, however, and if it were not for the chlorine content, the moisture of a covered swimming pool would be ideal, for sub-tropicals do not necessarily need full light.

It is interesting that as you work through the range of plants for a conservatory in your mind's eye, so the colour range of walls and/or upholstery to accompany them gets stronger. Temperate colours are soft, Mediterranean ones become sharper and clearer. Tropical colours are bright and really sing out, with wild patterns to match the leaf shapes of the accompanying plants.

The large conservatory perhaps makes the most ideal transition from inside to out, particularly in an unpredictable temperate climate. Well conceived, however, it can become adaptable for all sort of occasions. Its character can be of the garden creeping in, or, conversely, of the living room moving out. Pavings, the styling of furniture, colours, as we have seen, and plants all providing a relaxing and pleasant ambience. And that is really what it is all about – however you do it.

This beautiful, traditional conservatory provides a summer dining room that is right in the garden, for when the double doors are open, late evening fragrances waft inwards. In winter, such an extension would warm up quickly in the sun.

FURTHER READING

Betjeman, John,
Ghastly Good Taste, London, 1986

Boardman, John (ed.),
The Oxford History of Classical Art, Oxford, 1993

Boardman, John, Griffin, Jasper, and Murray, Oswyn (eds.),
The Oxford History of the Classical World, Oxford, 1986

Brookes, John,
Room Outside, London, 1990

Brown, Jane,
Gardens of a Golden Afternoon, London, 1990

Church, Thomas,
Gardens are for People, London, 1955

Crook, J. Mordaunt,
The Greek Revival, London, 1995 (rev. ed.)

Cunliffe, Barry,
Fishbourne – A Roman Palace and its Garden, London, 1971

Cunliffe, Barry,
Rome and Her Empire, London, 1994

Dickson, Elizabeth,
The English Garden Room, London, 1988

Ellis, Alice Thomas,
A Welsh Childhood, London, 1990

Etienne, Robert,
Pompeii – The Day a City Died, London, 1992

Fleming, Honour, and Pevsner, Nikolaus,
The Penguin Dictionary of Architecture,
Harmondsworth, 1980

Fowler, Peter,
The Garden Room, London, 1985

Gibbs, J. Arthur,
A Cotswold Village, London, 1983

Gilliatt, Mary,
Period Decorating, London, 1990

Koppelkamm, Stefan,
Gardens and Winter Gardens of the 19th Century, London, 1985

Krasner, Deborah,
Celtic, London, 1990

Lees-Milne, James,
Diaries 1942-1945, London, 1995

Lind, Carla,
The Wright Style, New York, 1990

Price, Eluned,
The Winter Garden, London, 1996

Radice, Betty (ed.),
The Letters of the Younger Pliny, Harmondsworth, 1969

Russell, Vivian,
Gardens of the Riviera, London, 1985

Shewell-Cooper, W.E.,
God Planted a Garden, London, 1977

Steer, and White,
Atlas of Western Art History, London, 1994

Thacker, Christopher,
The Genius of Gardening – The History of Gardening in Britain and Ireland, London, 1994

Thompson, Flora,
Lark Rise to Candleford, Oxford, 1939

Trevelyan, G.M.,
Illustrated English Social History, Harmondsworth, 1964

Walker, Winifred,
All the Plants of the Bible, London, 1958

Wilson, Michael I.,
The English Country House, London, 1980

INDEX

ACKNOWLEDGEMENTS

Grateful thanks for all their advice, time, trouble or support in one way or another are due to:

Carol Anderson, Senior Museums Officer, Oxfordshire Museums;
Thea Backhouse; Matthew Bates;David Clargo; Richard Collins;
Brother Benet Conroy, De La Salle Order, Oxford;
Nicola Drysdale, National Trust; Shirley du Boulay;
Ray Inskeep, formerly Lecturer in Prehistoric Archaeology,
Oxford University;
Dr Schuyler Jones, Director, Pitt-Rivers, Museum, Oxford;
Linda Lyne, Head of Classics, St Edward's School, Oxford;
Alan Marmion; Charles O'Brien, National Trust;
Jo Smith and Philippa Young.

PICTURE CREDITS

Gustavo de Almeida Ribeiro 150–5 (Jacques Auray, Yves Lefebvre)

Arcaid/Reiner Blunck (Glenn Murcutt) 163 top, Jeremy Cockayne 204, 216–7 (Pierre D'Avoine Architects)/Mark Fiennes 174–179 (Patrick Gwynne)/ Kurwenal, Prisma 15/Bill Maris, Esto 24/Alberto Piovano 164,194–5

Tim Beddow 102, 142–149 (John Pawson)

Bridgeman Art Library 11, 13

John Brookes 6, 16, 17, 22 top, 29 top, 94 top, 193, 196, 197, 206, 208

Simon Carnachan 163 below, 165 (Carnachan Architects Ltd)

Clive Frost 134 (Derek Frost)

Garden Matters 23

Garden Picture Library/Gil Hanly 27, 162, 166–173 (Ted Smythe, Mr & Mrs Faesenkloet)/Ron Sutherland 187

Robert Harding Syndication/IPC Magazines/Andreas Von Einseidel 5, 67–71, 133, 203 below/Marianne Majerus 93 top, 97, 99 top/Fritz Von Der Schulenburg 57 below, 95, 98, 99 below, 191, 192, 199/Tony Timmington 93 below, 96

Jerry Harpur 19 (Hestercombe), 22 (Folly Farm), 24–5 (Raimond Hudson, Johannesburg), 64 & 58–9 (The Hunting Lodge, Nicky Haslam), 99 right –101 (Sheila McQueen), 210 & 212–3 (La Casella), 26 & 213 (Felicity Mullen, Johannesburg)

Interior Archive/Derry Moore 73, 74 below & 75 (David Hicks), 180-185 (Oliver Messel)/Fritz Von Der Schulenburg 9, 18 & 32–7, 223 (Mlinaric, Henry & Zervudachi Ltd), 46–51 (David Hicks), 55 (Janet Fitch), 57 top (Jill de Brand), 74 top & 77 (David Hicks), 92 (Mlinaric, Henry & Zervudachi Ltd, Arabella Lennox-Boyd), 118–123 (Miguel Servera), 135 (Christophe Gollut), 136–141, 220 (Sandra Cooke), 156–161 (Ken Turner), 186 & 218 (Marston & Langinger), 190, 198–9, 200, 205, 207 (Jill de Brand)/Christopher Simon-Sykes 28, 29 below & 39–41 (Gervase Jackson-Stops), 30, 58, 60–3 & 65 (The Hunting Lodge, Nicky Haslam), 80–5 (Brian Bantry)

Andrew Lawson 42–45 (Gervase Jackson-Stops)

Sheila & Oliver Mathews 54, 221 (Pashley Manor), 208–9 (Cleveland House), 211 (Barnsley House)

The National Trust/Peter Baistow 202/Stephen Robson 90 below, 91/Geoffrey Frosch 86–9/Robert Truman 90 top

Jaap Oepkes 124–8 (Hannah Peschar)

Clive Nichols 1 & 8 (La Casella), 72, 76–7, 78, 79, 222 bottom (David Hicks), 94 below (Wendy Francis), 130 top & 131 (Hannah Peschar), 203 top & 215 (Keeyla Meadows)

David Parmiter 2–3 (Christopher Davies)

Eluned Price 7 & 132

Ianthe Ruthven 102–5 (Mathew & Maro Spender), 110–7, 222 top (Denny Wickham)

Elizabeth Whiting & Associates/Andreas Von Einseidel 129, 130 below/Jerry Harpur 22 below/Tim Street Porter 188–9, 214 (Tessa Kennedy)